"How you g_ _ _ _ _ _ _ _ _ you ain't right within . . ."

From the streets of South Orange, New Jersey, to the top of the charts, Lauryn Hill has burst onto the hip-hop/R&B scene with a sound and style that's getting noticed. Soulfully singing about the hard-won wisdom of emotional pain, the toxicity of bad relationships, the joy of motherhood, and much more, Hill speaks to everyone. And with ten 1998 Grammy nominations, she's being heard. *The Miseducation of Lauryn Hill* could be the most talked about album of the year—and will no doubt catapult her to legendary status.

lauryn hill

CHRIS NICKSON

St. Martin's Paperbacks

LAURYN HILL

Copyright © 1999 by Chris Nickson.
Cover photograph © Kuaku Alston.

ISBN: 0-312-97210-5

Printed in the United States of America

St. Martin's Paperbacks edition/April 1999

10 9 8 7 6 5 4 3 2 1

acknowledgments

This book would never have happened without the impetus of Madeleine Morel (true of all my books, but quite definitely the case here), and, as always, I'm very grateful to her. Also to my editor, Kristen Macnamara, who's worked very hard to make this into a swift reality. I sat and worked, but a whole cast of people helped in one way or another. Linda and Graham, whom I love very much, for their constant support. The cats, for comfort. Christian and Tonka, the lads in the basement, for banging and tea breaks. The Leeds United Internet list, for morning distractions. Friends, here and in England, who believed I could do it in the time allotted—Jonathon, Thom, Mike, Kevan, and others, thank you. Also, a shout out to Lauryn herself. The writing and research of this took me back to albums I hadn't played for a little while, to rediscover the joys of Aretha Franklin, the sublime Al Green, Stevie

Wonder, Marvin Gaye, Ann Peebles, Curtis Mayfield, Sly and the Family Stone. Absolutely brilliant stuff, and their songs form the real soundtrack to the book, at least in my head.

For material, I'm deeply indebted to the following articles: *Interview*, "Lauryn Hill and Maxwell," February 1998; *Harper's Bazaar*, "Capital Hill," by Daisann McLane, April 1, 1998; *Time*, "Songs in the Key of Lauryn Hill," by Christopher John Farley, September 7, 1998; *St. Louis Post-Dispatch*, "Sweeter the Second Time Around," by Alan Sculley, August 22, 1996; *Entertainment Weekly*, "Lauryn Hill, Cool and Committed," by Tiarra Mukherjee, June 28, 1996; *Vibe*, "Fugees: All 4 One," author unknown, March 1996; *Los Angeles Times*, "Q&A/Wyclef Jean," by Cheo Hodari Coker, June 21, 1997; *Vibe*, "The Fugees," by Mpozi Tolbert, June/July 1996; *Minneapolis Star Tribune*, "Fugees Take Solo Flights," by Jon Bream, January 27, 1998; *Vibe*, "Haitian Wyclef Jean," by Kris Ex, 1998; *The Voice*, "50,000 join the Fugees," April 28, 1997; *Newsday*, "Cuisinart Pop," by Carol Cooper, June 22, 1997; *The Independent*, "Clef's Big Treble," by Emma Forrest, June 27, 1997; *Ebony*, "Lauryn Hill," by Melissa Ewey, November 1998; *Entertainment Weekly*, "Lauryn Hill," by Jeff Gordinier, December 25, 1998; *Entertainment Weekly*, "Hill Power," October 2, 1998; *Rolling Stone*, "Lauryn Hill," by Greg Kot, January 21, 1999; *Spin*, "Lauryn Hill," by Craign Seymout, January 1999; *Los Angeles Times*, "Her Truth is Out There," by Elysa Gardner, August 23, 1998; *The Washington Times*, "Singer Has Learned Musical Lesson," by Burham Wazir, October 4, 1998; *Los Angeles Times*, "The Legal Tangle of 'Miseducation,'" by Geoff Boucher, December 19, 1998; *Vibe*, "Deliverance," by Karen Good, August 1998; *Essence*, "High on the Hill," by Monifa Young, June 1998; *Entertainment Weekly*, "The Student Turns Out to be the Master," by David Browne, September 4, 1998; *Newsweek*, "Ms. Hill Gives Her Lesson," by Allison Samuels, August 31, 1998; *People*, review, by Amy Linden, August 31, 1998.

introduction

Ten Grammy nominations. An album that entered the *Billboard* chart at Number One, and sold more in its first week than anything by any female artist (that includes Madonna, Mariah, Whitney, *everybody*). Polls by writers and artists all around America named it as the record of 1998.

That's a pretty remarkable track record for something that was made more by accident than design. But life happens in moments—some of them good, some of them bad. For Lauryn Hill, the good have definitely outweighed the bad over the last few years. She's become the queen of hip-hop, the woman who's connected the kindred spirits of reggae, soul, and rap, and given it a new, exciting face.

With the Fugees she was the pretty face with the glorious voice, the icing on Wyclef Jean's cake as he created the music that seemed to be his personal vision of global hip-hop, of world music with a danceable beat.

What blossomed out of that astonished and enraptured everyone. Lauryn showed herself as a strong woman, a spiritual woman, a mother whose concern was not just for her own child—now two children—but for the entire world. On *The Miseducation of Lauryn Hill*, she created a record that was about love and about caring. It was an antidote to the slick R&B that filled the airwaves. It had songs with messages that went beyond sex and offered an alternative to the misogyny of so much of rap, where the women stand on the sidelines while the men preen and undertake their violent, macho games. Here was someone intelligent and articulate, someone who'd discovered the history of her music, her race, her gender, and was proud of it. "Doo Wop (That Thing)" sent a positive message that resonated throughout the entire album.

The melodies and the beats were impossible to resist. But perhaps that was only to be expected when the inspirations were the great soul albums by people like Marvin Gaye, Stevie Wonder, Al Green, and Sam Cooke—the people who'd inspired her to make music in the first place.

All of those artists did more than make music, though; they made *statements* throughout their careers. That was a lesson which Lauryn Hill had obviously learned. And she'd learned that you can be a black woman, speak out, and be taken seriously.

"I want to empower," she said. "I want to inform. I want to inspire. . . . My agenda is to make sure that we're taken care of, and educated, and healthy, and happy."

They're big goals, they're artistic goals, but she has the power to achieve them. With the Fugees, she scored the biggest-selling album in hip-hop history with *The Score*, which sold seventeen million copies around the world in 1996, on the back of the remake of Roberta Flack's "Killing Me Softly With His Song," which was *the* hit of the summer. She became a superstar, part of a trio that put the creative back into the music (and brought reggae into the mix). A trio which didn't posture and brag but tried to offer something more positive than guns, violence, bitches, and ho's.

She was back in the news again as a single mother-to-be, refusing to sacrifice an unborn child to a career, and keeping her private life very private as she declined to name the father. Later, of course, the truth would come out. Her partner, who remains her boyfriend, was Rohan Marley, one of the sons of the great Bob Marley, the reggae legend.

With pregnancy came songwriting inspiration, first for Aretha Franklin ("A Rose is Still a Rose"), then gospel great CeCe Winans. The music flowed through her, words and melodies, as if they were coming from some other place. Without even trying, she had the bare bones of an album in front of her.

But she didn't take the obvious course, which would have been to bring in a superstar producer, a whole bunch of big-name guests and create "product." It would have moved off the shelves, but it wouldn't have given her the satisfaction she needed. If she was going to do it at all, she was going to do it right, do it her way. She was, after all, her own woman. That meant not only writing and singing, but arranging and performing. With real instruments and real musicians, not a string of samples, or some attempt to recycle the past as others had done with a lot of success.

Maybe it seemed contrary. But in a lot of ways it continued the ethos of the Fugees, where the band would do it all themselves, where Lauryn might strap on a guitar onstage to add to her singing.

The result, of course, was breathtaking. It was a widescreen look at her life, her philosophy, her chance to stand up and be counted. And it was wildly successful, artistically and commercially. That was gratifying, but it was never the whole point of the exercise. She made the album she set out to make. It marked her as one of the most creative women on the scene—quite a tag to be given at the age of twenty-three.

Suddenly, she was perceived as a spokes-person, an icon, which was something she hadn't wanted. But with celebrity and success comes a price. "Once you stand for something, that means you have opposition. You have to be well prepared."

And Lauryn was nothing if not well-prepared. With one child, and another on the way, she was grounded in motherhood. She was mama and lover as well as artist. But those were only a few facets of her personality. Like anyone, she's many different people. There's the social activist, who set up the Refugee Camp Youth Project in 1996, using her initial fame to help inner-city kids. There's the daughter who still lives in the family home in South Orange, New Jersey, and stays in touch with her roots, close to the projects. (She bought her parents a house just down the street.) There's the student who virtually had her choice of colleges and went on to study history at Columbia in New York, even as she was starting to set the world on fire with the Fugees. There's the actress who played roles in soap operas and movies—as unlikely a forum as you might be able to imagine for the Lauryn Hill of the album. And then there's the woman with the shoe fetish, who might turn up in five-inch heels.

You don't need to try and reconcile all the parts. They exist, and together with a lot of other pieces, they make up the person known as Lauryn Hill. It's more a case of accepting her for who she is. She's not going to change for anyone; just put everything together in one body. The little girl who discovered her mother's old 45s in the attic and played them as if discovering something secret is still alive within her. The ghost of Bob Marley lives on in her children, as she perpetuates and adds to a musical dynasty, and draws herself close to it—her album was recorded at Marley's Tuff Gong Studio, at 56 Hope Road, in Kingston, Jamaica, which over the years has heard some of the most inspirational words and music in the world.

In the wake of successful solo albums by all three members (as well as a book by Pras, *Ghetto Superstar*) the future of the Fugees remains in doubt. Everyone talks a good game about a new album in '99, and there's no doubt the label would love a follow-up to *The Score*. It would be an automatic multi-platinum hit, but Lauryn's tour would seem to indicate she won't be in the studio with the others anytime soon. It seems debatable how much they're even speaking. Although she counseled people not to take her lyrics literally, there were some phrases which could be interpreted as disses to Wyclef and Pras. Had they bought into the publicity? Were they playing the game they supposedly despised?

One thing that can never be doubted about Lauryn is that she's kept it real. These are her experiences, hopes, fears, desires, joys, and sorrows, all laid out on five inches of shiny plastic. They're the prism through which she sees the world, and makes music which she hopes will include and connect people, rather than exclude them from each other. But bringing things together is what love is all about.

Is she the visionary so many believe her to be, the person Chuck D of Public Enemy has described as "Bob Marley for the twenty-first century"? Is she the icon that journalists have made her out to be—someone with the ability to change the face of music, to make us feel better about life, about ourselves and each other?

Maybe. But the better question to ask is: how can anybody be those things other than by accident? No one can deliberately set out to be those things. They either happen or they don't. Connections are made, inspiration comes, things flow, and people respond. Some people make music that transcends time, and for others, it's strictly of the moment, the here and now. Lauryn's goal is much more realistic and achievable: "I want my music to touch real people. I'm still trying to figure myself out, like most people . . . because I'm still living and learning."

These days, the expectations that have been put on her are the kind that no one should have to bear. She broke ground with the Fugees (and in the new light, her role in that band has been reassessed), and now, with *The Miseducation of Lauryn Hill* she's taken a giant step forward, for herself and for all women in hip-hop—indeed, for all women in music. "They'll never throw the genius title to a sister," she complained. "They'll call her 'diva' and think it's a compliment. It's like our flair and vanity are put before our musical and intellectual contributions."

She's become a contender, not just as a female artist, but as an artist, period. The girl who used to be known as L-Boogie has matured into the woman known as Lauryn Hill. She's grown into her name, and she wears it with maturity and a certainty that it's hers.

It's a long way from playing Off-Broadway, or being on the soaps or in *Sister Act 2: Back in the Habit* to *The Miseducation of Lauryn Hill*, but that's what growing up is all about.

She's found her path; she's established herself. What she's gained on her journey can never be taken away from her. Her children, her music, her sense of self.

These days, Lauryn is in an enviable position. She speaks, and people listen. She appears, and people want to know why she's there. "I'm very happy. With a foundation, with a good man and a child, and a family— and I don't have the fear of losing my job. You know how in the office space people are sometimes hesitant to be vocal 'cause they could be fired for what they say? The only person who can fire me is God."

God. It's a word that comes up often when Lauryn speaks. She's filled with the spirit. Maybe not in the traditional sense, but she understands that without God in her life, there's nothing. All things flow from God. Her God might not be the traditional image of the man with the long white beard, but it's strong in her mind, her thoughts, her life. She's spiritual, and she understands that a closeness with God is something that's necessary for her. The blessings have flowed her way, and for that she's truly grateful.

Whether she wants it or not, Lauryn Hill is a star. The mantle has been thrust upon her, and she can't just ignore it. Instead, she's using it, to shine a light into the dark corners, to do her part to right wrongs and overturn injustices. She's ready to see in the new century, to be an active and vocal member of her generation, her gender, and her race—and that's the human race.

She has an audience, a constituency. In America, hip-hop long ago moved beyond the inner city to cement its popularity in the suburbs. Almost seventy-five percent of hip-hop albums these days sell to white kids. And not just boys, the girls buy them in equal numbers. The people listening to Lauryn, the more than three million who've shelled out money for her album, cross racial and sexual lines.

Some of those will have come to it from the Fugees, others curious after hearing "Doo Wop (That Thing)." A few will have been convinced by all the glowing reviews in the press. However they came to it, they've heard the message.

She's been lauded and applauded, feted and waited on. The ten Grammy nominations are lovely, but they're a bonus, not the whole meal. In a life taken seriously, the platinum albums and the awards can never mean that much. It's the basic things, the human things, and the artistic endeavor that really matter. And it's in those that Lauryn Hill has succeeded the most.

She's given birth three times, twice to living,

breathing children, and the third time to a record that speaks of her, of everything within and something which lets her out. All three are the product of love, of time, care, and energy, and all three have come from the heart and the soul.

Maybe she will be the future of hip-hop. Maybe she's already pointed the way to the next century. Only time can be the real judge of that. Certainly very few have connected the dots between past and present the way she has, and you have to know your history before you can move ahead (as she, a former history major, knows only too well). In the past, there is understanding, a chance to learn. In twenty-three years, Lauryn Hill has learned a lot. And every day brings more knowledge to be absorbed, to be used, and to be passed on. Lessons of the heart, lessons of the mind; they're all important. She may still be young, but that doesn't mean she can't teach, that she can't hold up a true mirror to society where it can see itself, and try to heal all the wounds that have been tearing it apart for so long.

At the bottom, we all live in one world. When Rodney King asked, "Can't we all just get along?", it was a big question. Maybe the answer isn't easy, but if Lauryn Hill and her music can help show some small piece of the path to reach that goal, then it'll be important, and lasting.

one

South Orange, New Jersey, seems like one of many small suburban towns that have sprung up within commuting distance of New York City. Manhattan stands across the water, some forty minutes away by car. Closer to home, the urban sprawl—which has become the urban decay—of Newark has spread almost to the doorstep.

In South Orange, the houses, wood or brick, look comfortable, homey, and the very image of the American suburban idyll, where every family owns its own place, and the children are raised in peace and security. The lawns are cared for, the grass cut, and flower beds planted. The white picket fences gleam. In summer the long days seem endless to the kids who play in the neighborhoods.

But the people who originally settled the suburbs have moved further out. These days it's only exurbia, as far away from the cities as possible in new developments, that offers a traditional, Norman Rockwell-lifestyle. It's been a couple of decades since urban life invaded the suburbs. Where wasteground once stood, there are now tower blocks of public housing, cheek by jowl with the proud houses. The old lines became blurred, and then faded altogether.

Lauryn Hill grew up, and still lives, on one of these suburban South Orange streets. The brick house echoed with the sounds of her and her older brother, who was six years old when she came into the world on May 26, 1975. It was a safe place, the door open in summer for the neighborhood kids to come and go, the grass watered to a rich green. But if you stood in the attic and looked out of the window, you could see one of the public housing blocks, no more than a few hundred yards away. Urban reality was right on the doorstep.

"I remember looking out this window," Lauryn recalled, "and there was a certain time of day when the sun used to shine on those buildings, and they used to look like gold. Beautiful. And I'd bug, 'cause I knew they were full of wild people, kids stickin' up each other. But when something is at its worst, there's always something beautiful there too." There were two worlds for young Lauryn, the one her family inhabited, where things were clean and bright and cheerful and life was lived with zest and energy, and the one she would walk to, where the tenements seemed to be neglected, and hope had been scrubbed out of the color scheme.

It was the difference between the haves and the have-nots, and Lauryn Hill grew up as one of the haves. Her parents encouraged her. They educated her. "When I was a very little girl I wanted to be a superstar/lawyer/doctor. I had an agenda," she remembered. The possibilities were open to her. There would be school, and then college. She could achieve whatever she wanted to achieve. The future was limitless.

But the projects also beckoned to her, with their edge of real life. She'd ride her little pink bicycle over there and hang with the kids in the playground. And even there she became known. Not for her background, but because she happened to be the baddest gymnast around. "I got my reputation 'cause I could flip. I was a huge tomboy, and I used to do backflips over there in the projects."

But she could always leave and go home to the brick house a few streets away, where life was very different. Both she and Malaney, her older brother who'd go on to become a lawyer, had their own rooms. There was a garden where they could play, not just acres of concrete. The family might not have been rich, but there was enough money.

Valerie and Mal Hill didn't just have jobs, they both had *careers*. She was a high school English teacher, and he worked in the fledgling computer business during the day, and exercised his skills as a singer in the evenings. They were both outgoing people, always ready for fun.

"My father is the type of father who at a wedding would try to breakdance and embarrass us," Lauryn said happily. They had a good time. They danced, they joked, they sang, and they kept something of an open house for their children's friends. They were, she said, "very, very cool."

Lauryn had her room, but it was the attic where she spent much of her free time. It was the place where the worlds came together. She could gaze out of the window at the projects, so close and so far. Around her was the clutter of her parents' history, stored away there rather than thrown out, where the past met the present. And it was in the attic, when she was six years old, that she discovered Valerie Hill's large collection of 45 r.p.m. singles. The objects, black and shiny, with a large hole in the center, each carefully packed in its paper sleeve, took on a special resonance for her, even before she ever played them.

Music had always been around the house, ever since she was born. Her father would rehearse his nightclub act, singing soul music from the fifties and sixties, the sounds of Atlantic, Motown, Stax, and all the other, smaller soul labels. Her mother would join in. There were new records playing on the stereo, more music on the radio, and *Soul Train* on the television. But when Lauryn first played one of the 45s on a record player in the attic, it was as if a whole new world had opened up before her.

"There was something sacred about those old records," she said wistfully. "They meant so much to me, and they kind of had a lot to do with the soundtrack of my life."

On the other side of the Hudson River, the hip-hop sound was just beginning to take shape. Up in the Bronx, deejays were spinning and scratching, the dancers were learning how to break, and MCs were getting on the microphone and rapping. It was all coming together into a completely new sound, one that would change the world. The Sugarhill Gang released "Rapper's Delight" and it turned into a massive national success. Kurtis Blow was starting out. And the new music, known as rap, was blowing away disco in New York.

A musical revolution was going on not far from home, but in suburban New Jersey, the young Lauryn Hill was slowly discovering the past. The sweet soul music that had moved her parents was moving her, too. The voices of Marvin Gaye, Al Green, Stevie Wonder, Aretha—every record offered a delight. And then there were the male-female duets: "I have a couple of all-time favorites," she said, "Donny Hathaway and Roberta Flack, Marvin Gaye and Tammi Terrell."

It all had a huge effect on her. Suddenly, instead of children's songs or the latest hits she heard on the radio, Lauryn was singing real soul music—and doing it very beautifully. Music seemed to touch her, to bring something out in her that nothing else could. She was a bright girl—both the Hill kids were smart—but for her, music seemed to possess magic. Her mother's record collection seemed to unlock something in her, bring the music out of her. "Oh, my fabled record collection," said Valerie Hill. "At the time, I didn't know it would have such an impact on Lauryn. But I always felt she would somehow, some way be involved in music."

It was soul that touched her, but that wasn't her only musical love. Show tunes, standards, jazz, it was all in the mix. Maybe it was inevitable that the girl who loved showing off her gymnastic skills in the project playground, impressing the other kids, would put that showmanship together with music in some form.

But it didn't happen immediately, by any means. Music was her thing, but it stayed around the house. That was where she felt free to sing, to explore all the different musics, to get a strong grounding in black musical history. Lauryn came from a strong, proud culture, albeit one that had been ground down and oppressed for far too many centuries. But it had a history, a place to call its own in the world, and to Valerie and Mal Hill, it was important that their children were aware of where they came from and what their roots were so they could be proud of who they were.

That, of course, was only one part of Lauryn's education. Since Valerie Hill was a teacher by profession, she made sure that *every* facet of her daughter's schooling was thorough. She followed up on the homework, and made sure Lauryn was keeping up with her lessons and understood what she was learning. She also took her to the theater, to see plays, musicals, all manner of things. And it was there that the idea of becoming a performer first hit Lauryn.

"When she was a girl, I took her to see *Annie,*" Valerie Hill recalled. "Afterward, Lauryn asked if there could ever be a black Annie." It seemed to ignite a spark in the girl. Maybe she wouldn't be the black Annie—and certainly there hadn't been one up to that point—but maybe she could utilize her natural talents and do something on the stage.

There was certainly encouragement in the family. Both Lauryn and Malaney were raised to be all they could be, to explore the different sides of themselves and bring them out. There might not have been the money to get every lavish luxury advertised on television, but that was the only thing that was lacking. ''I wasn't raised rich,'' Lauryn would say. ''But I never really wanted the things that we didn't have. I think my parents instilled in us that we didn't need lavish things. As long as we had love and protection, we were always taken care of.'' And there was no shortage of that in the brick house in South Orange. The harsh real world may have been just down the street, but inside everything was safe and warm.

That Lauryn could sing, and sing well, was well-known to her family, and in time it became known to her friends, too. And also to her brother and his friends. They were four years older, almost a generation for kids, so Lauryn didn't hang with them. But when they came to the house they could hear her, off on her own, singing. One of Malaney's friends, Marcy, took particular note of Lauryn's talent. It would prove to be a turning point before too long.

Malaney and Marcy were both students at

Columbia High School, one of the most prestigious in New Jersey. It had a strong academic reputation. One of the kids who also attended Columbia High went by the name of Prakazrel Michel, known to everyone as just Pras. His family had moved from Haiti to escape the bloodshed and misery caused by the Duvalier family, Papa Doc and his son, Little Doc, who ran the country like a private fiefdom, getting rich off the poverty of the population. For the Michels, and for the others who could get out, America seemed like a country of possibilities. Maybe the streets weren't paved with gold and maybe it wasn't packed full of opportunities if you were young and black, but it was better than the things they'd known in Haiti. They settled in the projects of Brooklyn, where many Haitians had gravitated, before moving out to South Orange. Pras grew up in New Jersey, where his father was a church deacon. He was very aware of his Haitian roots, but they were overlayed with America.

Like so many teenage boys, he'd fallen in love with hip-hop. Not just with the beats, but with the words, and the way they could be used, the things that could be expressed. Whether writing a rap or freestyling, he had the power to make it real. He could rhyme, he was fast; he was everything an MC needed to be.

In 1988, before hip-hop had become the sound of all America, it was the sound of the inner city. It was real, it was gritty, it was people talking about the life *they* lived. It was often angry and political. So it was no surprise that virtually every kid who could sling some words together wanted to be a rapper.

Getting a deal, though, was a different matter altogether. Even if you could talk the talk, you still needed someone good behind the wheels of steel, laying down some new, funky beats before you could really walk the walk. And most of all, you needed a good demo. Pras was fifteen. He had his stuff together, but he didn't have a good demo yet. But he had thoughts about something new. "I had this brilliant idea," he said, "that two girls and one nigga would be the bomb shit. Initially, it was me and this girl Marcy. We were supposed to get this other girl, but I didn't like her attitude."

Marcy, however, remembered Malaney's sister, the little girl who could sing so well, and she said to Pras, "I know this other girl, but she's real young." At the time, Lauryn was twelve, not quite thirteen. "I was like, 'What?'" Pras recalled. But Marcy insisted on Lauryn's behalf. "This girl can sing," she said. "She's baaaad." So she came down to the studio ("He was after fresh meat," she'd joke years later), and sang perfectly. It was exactly what Pras needed.

Or what he thought he needed. The record companies didn't seem to agree. But Lauryn had been up for it, and, intrigued with the possibilities, she remained up for whatever might come. They decided to call the new outfit "Time."

That was typical of her at the time. She was certain that there was nothing she couldn't do if she put her mind to it. For the most part, that was a good, and very positive attitude, but one time it did get her into some serious trouble. "A bunch of us went swimming and she swore up and down she could swim," said her friend, Miriam Farrakahn. "I mean, she was trying to tell us how to swim. We were like, 'Okay, let's see how you dive.' We threw her in and she almost drowned. Literally, almost drowned. I wanted to slap her!"

Maybe it was better to experience everything, even if it was dangerous, than to be scared of everything in life. And maybe it was better to believe you really could do anything you wanted than to back away from it all. Certainly, her experience in the water didn't put out Lauryn's fire for life and its possibilities.

Being in the studio with Pras, and having her singing praised, had given her confidence in her voice, and really fired her desire to perform. Not just as a singer—she wasn't about to put all her eggs in Pras's basket—but in every way possible. She'd been in plays at school and knew she was good there. It was enough to make her wonder how her talents would stack up in the real world. And there was only one way to find out.

With her mother's permission, Lauryn began traveling to New York to attend auditions. No one ever said it'd be easy, and it wasn't. But one trait Lauryn had been blessed with was persistence. If she failed at one audition, then the next one would go better. And indeed it did. There was a small part in an Off-Broadway production.

Being up on the stage, doing it professionally, was a major moment in her life. But she had no idea just how major it would be. In the audience was an agent, a man whose clients appeared on television and in the movies. He saw Lauryn act and knew she had potential. After the performance, he sought her out. All too often agents talk big, but talk is all that happens. And at the age of thirteen, Lauryn wasn't old enough to think of signing any contracts. With her parents in tow, she went to his office and sat down. He was realistic. He couldn't make any promises, but if she became his client, for his commission, he'd do what he could to get her work. If she wanted to pursue it, that was fine with both Mal and Valerie, but on one condition—that her school work would never suffer. That came before everything else, and there would be no negotiation on the matter. Lauryn agreed; she knew it was a given, anyway. So it was all set.

The agent proved to be as good as his word. He worked on Lauryn's behalf, setting up auditions and meetings. More than that, he wasn't just sending her after everything, but to jobs that had real possibilities for her. And pretty soon, in 1991, it all clicked. "She went on a few auditions and some go-sees, and the next thing you know, she had a part on a soap opera," Valerie Hill recollected. And not just any upstart soap at that, but one of the long-running daytime dramas, *As The World Turns*, which showed on one of the big three networks. Nor was it a single appearance; Lauryn had a small recurring role on the show. It was something most actresses would have loved, steady work with a paycheck. And it was the kind of prestige show and credit that would get her noticed, that would lead on to other things.

Granted, it meant that her days were full. Between school, work on the show, and her music, Lauryn basically had no free time. But she was happy, fulfilled, and contented. Nineteen ninety-one was a pivotal year for her. Suddenly she was on national television, which was a massive break in and of itself. But her music career also shifted into a higher gear. She'd been working with Pras on and off as he honed his sound, lending her sweet voice to his demos, and the two of them had also performed at contests around South Orange and Newark. They were beginning to make a little bit of a mark for themselves, but the sound needed more to set it apart from everyone else, to make it truly distinctive. And in 1991 that happened, when Pras's cousin, Wyclef Jean, came over from Brooklyn to lend a hand on one of the demo tapes. It was like magic had happened.

Wyclef Jean, born in 1970, was a couple of years older than his cousin, Prakazrel. He'd been born in Haiti and had lived there, one of the oppressed poor, until he was nine when his father, Pastor Jean Gessner Jean, fled with his family to America in search of a better life. "First thing: I don't think I was supposed to come to Earth," Wyclef would say later. "When my mother was in labor with me, they took forceps, went up inside of her, and pulled me out. So, in the back of my ears, I got two holes. If they didn't do that, I would have suffocated." His father was a Nazarene minister, but his grandfather was a priest in the voudou religion, the ancient rite that had come from Africa and found its real home in Haiti, a strange mixture of old ceremonies and Catholic religion. "There's all types of vibes that go on in the family," Wyclef said. "From religion, spiritual—some might call it mystical."

His first memories of the country he'd leave were of the rah-rah bands playing in the annual carnival. "I remember running on the side of the road as they passed through, playing with a bottle and a stick to keep rhythm. My family found me four hours later. Someone in the parade picked me up and made me a part of the throng, carrying me on their shoulders. I remember the sounds of the bells and the whistles, but I also remember the violence and the mystical power of the whole scene."

There was a power about it all, a sense of the past holding sway over the present, and tapped into with rhythms that became hypnotic. Field recordings of Haitian ritual music show how the rhythms start simply, then become more complex, drawing the listener in, and bringing him under its spell.

That was the good side of life. But under the dictatorship of Baby Doc, there was little hope for most of the people most of the year and few chances to forget the grinding poverty in which they lived. Shacks of materials thrown together, barely enough to eat, no money to spend on any kind of luxuries. If there was work, it was for wages that would still only supply the absolute necessities of life—the average worker made $3 US a *day*. By comparison, even the mean life in America looked rich. For Wyclef, life was made up of endless rounds of church and making music on whatever he could—discarded pieces of metal, pots and pans, even furniture. There was no future for him or his brother on the island. Life was hard, and you learned to live it. By the time he was seven, Wyclef already knew how to assemble a gun.

For a long time, Pastor Jean had been contemplating getting his family out—his wife and two sons, Wyclef and his older brother, Sam. Geographically, America wasn't far away. Plenty of other Haitians had made the trip and had prospered. There was decent housing and the chance to make a living wage, maybe even for the pastor to have a real church. Legally, however, America might as well have been the moon. There was no way for the family to get into the country under the auspices of the law. And if they went illegally, as so many had before, then they were risking everything. If they were caught on American soil, they'd be deported, right back to where they'd begun, and they'd never ever be allowed back into the U.S. So it took courage and determination on Pastor Jean's part to tell his family that they were leaving, that they'd risk all as illegal immigrants in the richest country in the world, where they might be able to find their small part of the American Dream.

The obvious place to go was Miami, in Florida. There was already a big Haitian community there, a network to help, shelter, and shield them, which they'd desperately need. No one in the family spoke English, only the Creole, a mixture of French (the French had once ruled Haiti), English and patois that was almost impenetrable to outsiders. So that was where the family headed in 1979. In Miami, Pastor Jean quickly found a job, although the fifty cents an hour he earned in the garment factory as sweated labor wasn't exactly a living wage. But his employers knew that he, and most of their work force, was illegal and took advantage of the fact. They took advantage in more ways than one. "They'd load immigrants and refugees in there and let them work for a month," Clef said. "Then they'd call Immigration, deport them, and let the next group come in." It kept the wages low, and the workers lived in constant fear of the INS finding them. By rights, Pastor Jean should have been caught with all the others who were rounded up. But on the day of the Immigration raid, something kept him away from the factory. He was lucky and escaped detection.

The only way to survive and get ahead at all

in this new country, the pastor decided, was to become a legal resident, and that was what he set out to do. Then, and only then, could he really do something for his family, and make sure they had a good education with which to make something of themselves. And the other thing was to get out of Miami. Further north the weather wasn't as warm and accommodating, but the emotional climate would be a lot more welcoming. As soon as he became a legal resident, had his green card, and social security numbers and all the correct documents for his family, the pastor moved them north, to Coney Island, in Brooklyn, New York. There was an apartment in the Marlboro Projects, cold weather and steamy summers to face, but at least now his family could move ahead. And there was still a sizeable Haitian community for support. Pastor Jean found a job that paid a living wage, and more importantly, he found a church that wanted him as its pastor, Flatbush Nazarene Church, in Brooklyn. "Outside the church, drug dealings would be going on. Inside, my father was preaching from the book of Revelation."

Life in the ghetto wasn't easy, but it seemed luxurious compared to what the family had known back in the Caribbean. There was violence, shooting, and gangs, but in many ways it remained safer than Haiti.

Wyclef and his brother had come to America speaking no English. His brother, smart in school, had quickly picked up the language. Wyclef took a different route. He learned from the words to songs, and more specifically, from the new rap music that was happening. "I actually learned English by listening to rap music," he admitted. "It's deep, because that's how a lot of foreigners learn, through rap or through television. It was funny, because I couldn't speak English, but I knew all the words to 'Rapper's Delight' and Kurtis Blow's 'The Breaks.' That's how I got introduced to hip-hop."

The boys grew. Sam Jean went on to college, where he'd eventually study law and become a member of the bar. Wyclef, younger and a little wilder, was taken with hip-hop, music that definitely came from the street, and as he hit his teens, he was starting to run with a bad crowd. He was at a point where his life could have gone either way. "When my brother was in college, I was on the streets," he recalled. "When he'd come home, there were certain areas he couldn't go. I had to take him. My brother is my direct opposite, but I always made sure he was protected, without him ever knowing." And Wyclef himself was protected. The spiritual power of his father and grandfather was in him. He had power. One night he was out and someone put a gun to his head. ''I said, 'You cannot shoot me. You are not authorized to shoot me.' '' The man with the gun ran instead. By the next day it had become a ghetto legend.

A ghetto legend could have been the fate of Wyclef Jean, and it might well have happened that way if it hadn't been for his mother. She knew how much music meant to him, and thought that if he was playing, rather than just listening, his energies might go toward something more creative. ''My mom got me my first guitar,'' he said. ''She geared me toward music.'' At home, in his room, Wyclef would listen to hip-hop, totally caught up in the music, which displeased his father. Actually, it was ''not just hip-hop, but anything that didn't say 'God' or 'Jesus is coming back.' Everything else, as far as he was concerned, was devil music. My father would whup my ass for playing rap. He couldn't understand English well at the time, but I had to play music in the house that sounded like Christian music to him. I could get away with listening to Pink Floyd's *Wish You Were Here*, I could listen to the Police, but when he heard a rap beat, he'd say 'Turn that off!' ''

After getting his guitar and learning to play, Wyclef began working on his own songs. He took part in his high school jazz orchestra, where he heard music by Coltrane and Mingus, and improved his own instrumental chops by copying people as diverse as Hendrix, Muddy Waters, and the classical guitarist Segovia. He'd seen and experienced far more than most kids his own age, and he thought he had something to say, something important about rights and about injustice. His writing, along with his singing and playing, improved the more he worked at them. The people he played his music for were encouraging. He was working in the hip-hop field, but he was bringing in other original ideas. It was different. And on the side he also had a funk band, inspired by Parliament and Funkadelic.

In 1987, when he was seventeen, he decided to start putting his material on tape. At the very worst, it would be there to hear. At best, something might happen to get him out of the ghetto. His brother had taken the academic way, but that wasn't going to work for Wyclef. He needed to forge his own path. But the music he wanted to sing didn't sit well with his father. "It got really bad when, at seventeen, I started going to the recording studios and sneaking in the house later at night through the roof, and he'd be waiting for me in the dark with a thick belt. It got to the point where he would nail the front door shut so I would freeze to death outside in order to learn that

Jesus Christ was the way.'' But nothing was going to keep Wyclef Jean from his music. He'd had a taste, he knew its power, and he was part of it.

Wyclef knew that his cousin, Pras, was a rapper, and that his band was doing quite well around South Orange. The two sides of the family saw each other regularly. At that time, Wyclef, who was older, seemed to be the one who was likely to make it first. ''I always used to meet up with Clef at church in Jersey,'' Pras recalled. ''He would say, 'Yo, man, when I get a record deal, I'm gonna put you on board.' Then one day, he came to the studio and dropped his vocals on one of our tracks.'' It was exactly what they needed. Innately, Clef brought in the Haitian and Jamaican influences to the music, giving it a kick well out of the ordinary. ''The producer we were working with at the time was like, 'Y'all need to be a group.' We said, 'Fuck it—I'd rather deal with my own family anyway.' Clef decided it was time to end his funk days and concentrate on this new sound.

And that was how the Fugees were born.

two

They weren't exactly the Fugees at that point, however. Back then, in 1991, the name they chose was "Tranzlator Crew." Then it was amended to "Fugees (Tranzlator Crew)," a sort of midway point on the road to just the "Fugees." Fugee was short for refugee, which referred to the plight of so many people in the world, and most specifically, to Haitians themselves, for whom the term "refugee" had often taken on a derogatory connotation in America. Since the band contained two Haitians, reclaiming the term was important, a badge to be worn with honor.

The three of them began to work together, crafting new material and excited at the turn it was all taking. Instead of just being another hip-hop outfit from Jersey, albeit a good one, they were doing something quite new by adding Haitian rhythms, Jamaican dancehall, and ragga to the mix. All three of them were strong on the mic; they could all sing and rap. Lauryn came across well as a rapper, giving out the image of a strong young woman with a positive message for other girls. And a positive message was important for all three of them. Hip-hop abounded with negativity, with stories of guns and people getting blown away, of drug dealing and women who were referred to as bitches and ho's. None of that would enter their music. Instead, they'd spread words of love, respect, of not backing down, but not being violent either; they all understood full well that violence was nothing more than a dead-end street.

They began playing their new stuff around Jersey, and it was well received. The Tranzlator Crew was developing a small following for their individual approach to music. There was enough recognizable hip-hop in there to get people into it, but also enough that was new and different to put them on a different level.

Playing show and finding their feet was one thing. Moving ahead from there was a different matter altogether. They were recording when they could, and slowly amassing equipment. Lauryn recalled that "Wyclef was so determined . . . I used to hit him off with whatever I could now and then, and he would buy another piece of equipment. Over time, he accumulated a complete studio." But it didn't mean anything if they couldn't get someone to listen to the tapes they were making. Pressing a CD themselves was out of the question. Not only did it cost too much, but how would they get it into people's hands? They were artists, not businessmen. They needed a manager to handle all that for them.

Finding one wasn't as difficult as they'd thought. From the shows they'd done, word had spread in the area. People were checking them out. Among them were representatives of a local production company formed by Khalis Bayyan, a former member of Kool and the Gang. He loved what he saw, and signed the Fugees. Maybe it seemed like a long jump from Kool and the Gang to the Tranzlator Crew, but Bayyan wanted to work with Lauryn, Pras, and Wyclef. The bottom line was that good music was good music, and this was good, and very innovative, music. And maybe from pop-funk to hip-hop wasn't as great a stretch as it seemed, anyway.

Bayyan proved himself very useful. He hooked them up with David Sonenberg, whose DAS Communications had been the manager of Meatloaf during his *Bat Out of Hell* days. It wasn't hip-hop, but it had been one of the biggest-selling albums ever. That meant Sonenberg had clout. When he talked, people listened.

Bayyan set up an audition for the new band with Sonenberg. It was one of those curious coincidences. A few years before, Sonenberg had attended an amateur church production, where he'd been struck by a young singer with a very distinctive voice. Although he'd done nothing about it at the time, when Wyclef Jean stepped into his office, he recognized him as that young man. While Sonenberg listened, Clef played his acoustic guitar and Lauryn sang John Lennon's "Imagine." They performed a few raps, freestyling for the man. Sonenberg was impressed. Hip-hop wasn't his field, but he could sense that this went way beyond that; the potential was enormous. He signed them.

Having management was hugely important. It made them real, made them viable. And Sonenberg got to work on their behalf immediately, getting the Tranzlator Crew demos out to a number of labels and setting up small, intimate showcases that would show every facet of the band, from Lauryn's seductive voice to Jean's politics. The demo got some interest from one small label, Ruffhouse, a small imprint of the giant Columbia label.

Ruffhouse was run by two guys from Philadelphia, Joe Nicolo and Chris Schwartz, a pair with real credibility and ever greater success in hip-hop. They'd worked with Schooly D, one of the old-skool rappers; they'd discovered Cypress Hill; and they'd also been the driving force behind Kriss Kross, who scored a massive single with "Jump," which went all over the pop charts. Success breeds success, and Columbia created Ruffhouse for them to release the stuff they wanted; but they were selective about the artists they wanted to work with. As a team, Nicolo and Schwartz worked well together, the first geared toward production, the second toward promotion.

David Sonenberg got Nicolo to come to a Fugees showcase gig after he'd heard the demo. Live, the power and the presence of the three outweighed what they'd laid down on tape. Nicolo talked to his partner; they wanted them on Ruffhouse. The deal was signed, and the band went into the studio. For all of them, this was amazing. In just a few months since Clef came on the scene, things had moved at an incredible pace. Lauryn was barely sixteen at the time, still working on *As The World Turns*, though her character was being written out.

The initial work was undertaken at Bona Fide Booga' Basement in New Jersey, the studio owned by Jerry "Wonder" Duplessis, another Haitian and Clef's cousin on his other side, keeping it all within the greater Tranzlator Crew family. Duplessis played bass and guitar, although he wasn't featured on the album. The Crew knew the studio well—they'd made some of their demos there—and they felt comfortable doing all the pre-production work on the album there.

For Lauryn, it seemed to deepen the mad rush that her life had become. There was school, where she was holding up good grades, her work on the soap opera, and now nights and weekends in the studio, refining and polishing everything the band had done.

Few albums get made overnight. What you hear on a CD is the product of months, sometimes even years, of work. As a new act, the Crew didn't have too much money to work with, so the recording proper was done at House of Music, Inc. in West Orange, New Jersey, a stone's throw from home. Wyclef and Pras were responsible for some of the production, working with Rashad Muhammed, Brand X, Khalis Bayyan, and Stephen Walker in various combinations on various tracks. Over the summer of 1991 it all took slow, painful shape. It was like giving birth; some parts happened quickly and simply, others took forever to fall into place.

The Tranzlator Crew had their songs; in the studio they could use those as a foundation and build on them with programming and samples, as well as live instruments. Everything was built from the ground up. The only rule was that it all had to be real. And it was.

In the fall of 1991, as Lauryn began her junior year of high school, they delivered the completed album to the label. The band was thrilled with it. The first feedback from the suits who heard it was enthusiastic. And then there was silence.

Keeping up with everything was overwhelming for Lauryn. Having been on national television in her recurring soap opera role was a thrill, but on top of the band and school, it simply stretched her too far. She needed to be thinking ahead because college was on the horizon. This was the time she really needed to be getting her head down and studying properly, making the best grades she could, and cramming for the SATs. So when her character was written out of the show, she said goodbye to her time in front of the cameras with a mixture of sadness and relief. She hadn't been a star, but she'd been a presence, and she'd learned early that it wasn't that important. It was a job, like any other. You went in and did your best work, and then you went home again. Life would go on, whether she was on the show or not.

"I was fifteen years old, makin' my little money off the soaps," she recalled, and a lot of what she earned went straight back into the band. Emotionally, it was a lot more important to her than *As The World Turns*. Not having that extra commitment freed her up to focus more on the really important things in life. But all of a sudden, the business of music seemed to have ground to a halt. They were left waiting, not knowing what was going on. It was just business. And when might the record be released? No one was willing to say. It was open-ended.

That left the Tranzlator Crew, or Fugees (Tranzlator Crew) as they'd become known now, hanging. They were signed to a record label. They'd made a record they were proud of, delivered it on time and on budget, and now it was just sitting there. It was a frustrating time, sitting in limbo. With no product to sell, all they could do was keep playing the local places they'd been gigging before the contract had been signed. There was no moving on, or moving up.

Wyclef and Pras were unhappy, but they could retreat into the studio and do more writing. In that regard, there was always the future for them. But it left Lauryn without any artistic outlet, and she'd discovered enough to know that she needed something, some form of creativity in her life. Making music with anyone else was out of the question. She'd known Pras since eighth grade, and he and Clef were more than just homies, they were *family*. That left her other big option, which was acting. Her agent had been keen for her to do more work, and he set up auditions, which led to her acting in two movies, the first in 1992, the second in 1993.

King of the Hill was directed by Steven Soderbergh, who'd initially made his name in 1989 with *sex, lies and videotape*, which won stunning reviews from the critics, as well as first prize at the Cannes Film Festival, Best Film in the Independent Spirit Awards, and a nomination for Best Original Screenplay at the Academy Awards. All in all, it was a remarkable result for a directorial debut, and particularly for an independent film. From there he'd gone on to make *Kafka*, with English actor Jeremy Irons starring as writer Franz Kafka, in a film that seemed to generate nothing but disappointment from reviewers on its release in 1991.

King of the Hill would be his third feature, with Soderbergh himself writing the screenplay from A.E. Hotchner's book describing his own childhood in Depression-era St. Louis. The story was that of Aaron Kurlander (played by Jesse Bradford), a twelve-year-old boy who learns to grow up quickly. His family, consisting of his parents, himself and his brother, live in a seedy hotel. Then his mother is committed to a tuberculosis sanitarium, his younger brother is sent off to live with relatives, and his father gets a job as a traveling salesman. Aaron does well at school, and the other residents of the hotel become something of a family to him, as well as the people he encounters on the street.

It was another independent release for Soderbergh, and that meant that once again there would be few major names. Spalding Gray took a part, as did Karen Allen and Elizabeth McGovern, but they were the only real known quantities—and even they were hardly what anyone would call box-office draws. Lauryn had nothing more than a bit part, a few days of filming, but it was something to begin to satisfy the hunger to express herself.

With the crucially important SAT examinations coming up, it was perhaps just as well that there were just those few days of filming for Lauryn. Both Valerie and Mal Hill wanted her to concentrate on the tests, which would be far more important to her future than any film role. She took them and scored very high marks in every area, one of the top student scores that year at Columbia High. It seemed as if anything Lauryn undertook, with her mind set on it, she'd be successful.

The SATs, of course, led to college applications, and with her impressive scores, both her parents and her school counselors encouraged Lauryn to apply to the country's top schools, Ivy League and others. And that was exactly what she did. Her applications went off in the mail to Yale, Rutgers, Spelman, Columbia, and the University of Pennsylvania—an impressive collection made all the more impressive by the fact that Lauryn was offered a place at every one of her choices.

It was an embarrassment of riches, really. She could pick and choose. Yale had the prestige, but Spelman would connect her to Black history. However, she had to choose one of them, and in the end she opted for Columbia, which was in Manhattan. An important school, but still close to home, and close enough to keep her working with the band, which, apart from her education, was her main priority. Their career couldn't stay on hold forever; at some point Ruffhouse *had* to put out the album.

Finally, a release date early in 1994 was set, which would happen right as Lauryn began her second semester as a freshman at college. There was still plenty of time before that, including a summer after she'd finished high school, and she had no wish to be just sitting at home twiddling her thumbs. Once again, her agent came up trumps, landing her a small film role.

Sister Act 2: Back in the Habit wasn't exactly high art. It was being made solely to capitalize on the success of the original *Sister Act*, Whoopi Goldberg's comedy vehicle. As Whoopi described the sequel, "Deloris (her character, Deloris Van Cartier, otherwise known as Sister Mary Clarence) is back. The nuns are back. We got some priests. We got some intense kids. It's an all-singing, all-dancing, all-acting kind of thing." Along with Goldberg, people like Kathy Najimy and Maggie Smith returned from the first movie. The movie brings Deloris back from a career that's taking off in Las Vegas to pose again as a nun at an inner-city school and help get the troubled students into good enough shape to win an all-state choral competition. And it was one of those troubled inner-city kids, Rita Wilson, that Lauryn Hill played (there was another largely unknown young actress in the cast, too, by the name of Jennifer Love Hewitt). When it was released, late in 1993—after a pretty quick post-production turnaround—it didn't exactly get winning reviews. Nor was it that popular with audiences, only managing to gross $56.9 million (as opposed to $139.4 million for the original), a figure that the studio, Disney, considered disappointing.

At least it gave Lauryn more of a role than *King of the Hill*, and the chance to sing, as well as act, even if her abilities weren't seriously tested. And, for a budding actress, every additional line on the resume was a help for the future. It also helped fill that long summer gap between school and college. And *Blunted On Reality*, as the band had decided to call it, finally appeared in the stores early in 1994, a little more than two long years after they'd recorded the tracks. Finally, it seemed, Lauryn's life could really move ahead again.

three

It was never about the money. Too many peo-ple got into hip-hop so they could make money and live large. That was fine, it was one way out of the whole cycle of poverty that was the ghetto. But there was a lot more to life than what was in your bank account, or round your neck or on your wrist. You might be wearing a Rolex, but if you weren't aware of what time it really was, then you might as well be wear-ing a Timex.

If all you could do was talk about what a big man you were, the guns you carried, the women you'd mistreated, how you'd come up selling crack on the corner and were making money off that, then all you were doing was taking. What the Fugees (Tranzlator Crew) were about was going deeper.

It was about giving back, making people think, and addressing issues that didn't often see the light of day. Why were Haitians treated like boat people in America, Clef wanted to know. Why did black people seem to want to kill each other—not that some whites seemed to object to that too much. Why did it seem that being black in America meant you were often stopped by the police (and the band had recorded their album before the Rodney King trial in 1992)? And as for Lauryn, she was wondering why so many black men felt they had to disrespect black women, to refer to them as bitches and hos, to treat them as lesser human beings. They addressed the issues of race relations, the way blacks had been—and still were—exploited by the whites, and the idea that everything was going to be all right—because it obviously wasn't. This was about art and politics, about being willing to stand up and be counted, to say your piece without being shouted down, to respect yourself so that you could respect others. It was about history and sociology, and about the things that touched lives every day.

On its release, *Blunted On Reality* hit the *Billboard* R&B chart, at the bottom of the 100, set to climb to number 62. The first track "Nappy Heads" had been extracted as a single, and that slipped straight into the *Billboard* Hot 100, where it would peak at number 49.

In terms of chart performance, they didn't set the world on fire, but in an industry where thousands of records were being released every year, it was obvious that someone was listening. The total sales for the album were 130,000. Again, they weren't going to change the face of the business, but it was still respectable. It more than repaid the faith Ruffhouse had shown in them, and it meant that over one hundred thousand people were listening, and caring enough to spend their money on the record.

The people who were paid to listen to and write about music heard the album with a great deal of interest. Sure, some of it was quite derivative of the work Public Enemy had done, without the explosive backgrounds of the Bomb Squad. But there were other things going on that made it stand out and worthy of praise. They brought in a reggae element, which was definitely different, and then there was the simple Haitian guitar rhythm that floated behind ''Vocab.'' Dancehall and ragga were in there, making the whole thing into a real melting pot of black ideas and ideologies. Something was going on, and with some reservations about the overall production, and the sparseness of some of the tracks, the critics found a lot to praise in the Tranzlator Crew.

It all began with a manic introduction over churchy organ chords, leading into a poem by Lauryn, taking on the guise of a KKK member and the attitudes those people had toward blacks. Then the speakers exploded with "Nappy Heads," which echoed the same themes. It had the power of some of the best of Public Enemy; the three of them traded off on the mic, saying their piece about the state of the black race in America. Produced and arranged by Rashad Muhammed, Brand X, Wyclef and Pras, it utilized samples from Kool and the Gang's "Heaven at Once" and Earth, Wind and Fire's "I Think about Loving You," which was an interesting juxtaposition, taking elements of songs from bands known more for their dance material than anything political. It set the scene for what was to come lyrically. There weren't going to be any punches pulled. This was their shot, and they were going to take it. Pras, Clef, and Lauryn weren't sucker MCs; they had a lot to put across, and they were going to do it.

Lauryn, in particular, was something of a revelation. The little girl who'd sung backup on Pras's demo and joined him in Time had developed into a fully-formed rapper, as angry about the world as anyone else. She had a tough style, harder than almost any female rapper around, and she was unabashedly political, which certainly set her apart. No other woman in rap was talking about the same things as Lauryn.

The word might have been that the members of the band didn't use pot, and that *Blunted On Reality* meant being high on the positive possibilities of life, but the conversational start of "Blunted Interlude" was definitely about weed. It bought into a track built around a loop of bass and guitar, both played by Wyclef, with the programming by Rashad Muhammad. In a lot of ways it was the most disappointing cut on the album. The rhymes weren't particularly inspired, and the music didn't really move anywhere. What it did have working for it was a sung chorus that was obviously inspired by Jamaica. For the rest of it, it was nothing more than sub-Public Enemy, with ideas that had been explored a few years before. Produced by Clef and Pras, with co-production by Khalis Bayyan, it just didn't cut it, except for the chorus which stood out like a breath of fresh air.

"Recharge" took off on some spacy synth and singing before kicking in to the rap over the scratches from DJ Boy Wonder. This was mad with all manner of effects over keys—cell phones ringing, the sounds of the street. The street was what this was all about, and what it was like growing up in the ghetto. But that was just the starting point. It became a meditation on life, religion, and the positive possibilities once Lauryn was on the mic—it was really hard to believe that she was only sixteen when she'd recorded this. Then there was a very Haitian sung section in Creole before going back into the rap, with Pras showing his stuff. It seemed as if a lot of the most interesting things that were going on in this album were happening in the smaller spaces—the Haitian and Jamaican influence that brought melody into the whole. And when Clef took the mic, it could almost have been reggae band Blacjk Uhuru, with Sly and Robbie on the drums and bass behind them.

"Freestyle Interlude" was exactly that, with the sounds of car horns and a small crowd, guys trying to outdo each other as they rhymed, the whole competition broken up by the arrival of the cops, and ending with the sound of a car wreck.

After that, "Vocab" stood as something totally different from anything in hip-hop. No drums, no percussion, just Clef's acoustic guitar double under his thoughts about what it had meant to him to be Haitian in America. Written by Pras and Clef, this was their reality, their experience, and it was the sound of people speaking from the heart. People who'd lived everything they said, and who couldn't help but look at the country as outsiders. The simplicity of its sound brought the listener's attention just by being so spare. But it was more than that. It possessed something special, the kind of pair that keeps ears riveted, that makes them want to hear more. The guitar rhythm evoked Haiti. And when Lauryn came in, speaking her colleagues' words, asking what was wrong with the black man, dissing their sisters, it moved to another level. This was the sound of black womanhood standing up for its rights. It all came down to the fact that you couldn't believe in Babylon, as the white world was known in Rastafarian terms. There had to be unity, otherwise there was nothing.

After that, "Special News Bulletin Interlude," a supposed Jamaican news broadcast about blacks being killed (and also a shout out to the massives and the Yardies—the Jamaicans—who were all over New York and New Jersey), brought in "Boof Baf," where Clef continued to get to grips with the way Haitians had been treated in America, often mistaken for Jamaicans and told to get back to Jamaica. The keys, played by Khalis Bayyan, formed a funky pad for the rhymes to spring off. L took her time at the mic, but this time out she wasn't saying too much. Clef's ragga interlude was way cool. But after a promising beginning, it seemed to degenerate into standard hip-hop, with little to set it apart from a hundred other hopefuls.

"Temple" was a different matter altogether.

Religion wasn't something that was often addressed by the hip-hop community, but it had been a big part of their upbringing for all the band, most particularly Wyclef, for whom fundamental Christianity had meant more oppression. Written by Clef and Pras, and produced by them with co-production by Khalis Bayyan, the man they all referred to as their "father figure," everything really came together again here with a one-drop reggae bassline under some synthesized horns that could almost have come of an old Studio One Coxsone Dodd-produced track made in Jamaica in the late sixties. Lauryn started off in a dancehall style, trying to figure out how Christians could use the N-word, and how religion could cause diversity rather than unity. Then Clef took over, giving something of his story, how he got into hip-hop, and how his father had given him a bad time about it. Pras and Clef together took it on a spiritual detour. Again, this was a track that offered something different from what had become the accepted mainstream of hip-hop. The rhymes were there, no doubt, but it was what was going on behind them that piqued the interest. The Crew could mix hip-hop and reggae seamlessly into a whole that worked. It borrowed from dancehall, the reggae genre that had borrowed from hip-hop, which had its beginnings in the Jamaican DJs of the early seventies, coming full circle. It moved the vocal speed up several notches but never aped dancehall. If anything, the vibe was relaxed.

You couldn't say the same for "How Hard is It?" where the operative word was quite definitely hard. Produced, arranged, and written by Clef, Pras, and Khalis Bayyan, this was street-tough. Yes, it was real, but this wasn't what the Crew did best. The world didn't need another Public Enemy when the original was still at the top of its game. Braggadocio really didn't suit them, and the comparison of mics to guns was already getting pretty old and tired. The most interesting thing was the jazz middle eight from Lauryn, over a sax line that played the old standard "Take the A Train." Coltrane was name-checked, and the sax on the outro echoed some of his work in the early sixties—respect was due, and it was paid. Again, there were interesting things happening, but somehow they got a little lost and possibly ignored in the overall bombast of the track, and also in the thickness of the production, where even the bass was muddy and not the loud, clear beast it needed to be to kick something that wanted to be as hard as this.

"Harlem Chit Chat Interlude" was Rashad Muhammad's little piece, with street talk from Clef, Pras and Jean over a tuba bass, the sound of the subway, and some jazz piano.

"Some Seek Stardom" had Muhammad on bass, Larry Stokes on guitar, and Khalis Bayyan on the Hammond organ, creating some soulful Southern music, with a gospel feel under the rhymes. The sample came from Aretha Franklin's version of Paul Simon's "Bridge Over Troubled Waters." The song was a diss to those who pursued stardom but turned their backs on their communities, with L sounding melodic as she rapped. The music was soulful, which was apt since this was about what happens to people's souls. She even got into some beautiful jazz singing midway through, more Ella Fitzgerald than Queen Latifah, an idea picked up by Bayyan's soprano sax on the fade.

Wyclef and Pras wrote, arranged, and produced "Giggles," with co-production by Bayyan, and some live drums underneath it all by Derrick Darling. The keyboard bounced funkily, and the whole band came in on the chorus—the idea of a chorus in hip-hop seemed to be something of a Crew trademark, picked up on the old skool ideas of Grandmaster Flash. But the whole thing had a sense of lightness and fun with the funk (a track called "Giggles" couldn't exactly be hard, anyway).

"Da Kid From Haiti Interlude," penned by the trio, taped as if it was from the street, was a little slice of life that permeated the whole album. It was set at a school, featuring a girl who didn't want to talk to a Haitian, just because of where he was from.

In many ways that made the perfect introduction to "Refugees on the Mic." We're all refugees in our own way, on our own journeys from one place to another, be it spiritually, emotionally, or physically. Once again it was produced by Clef and Pras, with help from Bayyam, and written by the two Haitians along with Lauryn. In some ways, it was vaguely reminiscent of Lou Reed's "Walk on the Wild Side." It began with Clef stating how Haitians were treated in America, when they were just trying to get by, and get a life, when there was none for them back in Haiti. And it was true that islanders—all islanders—were treated like second-class citizens. They wanted to live, to make it, and all too often that meant resorting to crime. And for some of them, if they were arrested, that meant deportation as illegal immigrants. That was real life, and it was tragic that it had to be that way. Lauryn added her rhymes, even though she was not Haitian, but it wasn't where she was from that was the issue, it was speaking out against injustice and against prejudice.

"Living Like There Ain't No Tomorrow," by Pras and Wyclef, produced by the two of them and Jerry Duplessis at the Booga' Basement Studio, worked over a wobbly keyboard figure. It was preaching against hedonism. You couldn't live like there was no tomorrow. Every action has consequences, and they need to be considered, whether in love, sex, money, spirituality, or other ways. And if you lived in your own personal Sodom and Gomorrah, then you'd pay for it somewhere down the line— whether in this life or the next. There was violence, and gunshots, but this was Clef and Pras looking back to their backgrounds, and standing on the pulpit.

"Shouts Out from the Block," rounded out the problem proper. Pras gave props to everyone who'd supported the band, together and individually, in the past in Brooklyn and in Jersey. Then to the brothers from every part of the country, in a spirit of unity, and those from the Caribbean and Africa, before Clef took the mic to give his thanks. It did go on a bit, however, and more than six minutes had passed before L-Boogie got onto the mic.

And that was it, the Fugees, as they were starting to call themselves then, in the house. Or that was almost it, except for one last track, a remix of "Nappy Heads," the PE style opener that was taken and completely deconstructed by Salaam Remi. All too often, a remix is even denser than the original, adding the remixer's ideas, and using the original track as the backbone of it all. This took "Nappy Heads," or at least the rhymes, as a springboard, but stripped the music way, way back, as if it had taken off twenty layers of suffocating winter clothing. It began with Clef singing, then a trumpet line, a straightforward beat, then keyboard chords underpinning it all. It sounded a lot less American, and brought out the natural island flava of the track that had been hidden before, and it didn't use any samples. Along with "Vocab" it was the real standout of *Blunted On Reality*, and Remi would also do a remix of that track, adding a few subtle elements, that would eventually appear on *Bootleg Versions*. The two would circulate in clubs and on the radio for a while, and help keep the flag flying until 1996, when *The Score* would appear.

All in all, *Blunted On Reality* might have achieved decent commercial success, but it was the sound of a band that had yet to fully find its own voice. There were snatches of it, indications of the possibilities, but overall it didn't take enough risks. It was still too much like too many hip-hop bands out there, at least musically. Worse, by the time it came out, it sounded dated, as people like Wu-Tang Clan and Cypress Hill had done a lot to change the face of hip-hop. "The production on our last album was wack," Wyclef would say later.

"But for the next album, we're not working with the same people. Our next album is gonna be the bomb."

That was positive thinking, looking ahead. But for now, this was the album they had to support, even as they continued to work up new material and look ahead. Shows were set up—there was a tour after Lauryn's freshman year at Columbia was over—and the Fugees took it on the road. There they could show just how different from other hip-hop bands they really were. This wasn't an outfit working the mics to a pre-recorded tape or the sounds of a DJ. This was a real band, with real instruments, which made them one of the very few in hip-hop to do that. Clef would play the guitar, the bass, or the keyboard. L could pick up a guitar, and they could switch off from each other. They weren't limited by some backing track; they could let the show go where it wanted, and include all kinds of things, anything they wanted.

They'd served their time playing small local shows. Cracking it a bit bigger was something new to them, and they almost blew it. For some reason, they decided to take the stage in color-coordinated outfits that did none of them any favors. And, to top it all off, their first few shows in '94 had them indulging in some very goofy routines. For a band that wanted to come across as totally real, it all smacked very heavily of showbiz and complete artifice, which wasn't the image they wanted to put across. For every step forward, there seemed to be another one back. All that, however, was soon sorted out, and the Fugees began kickin' it, looking like themselves, being themselves, and turning in some incendiary performances that got people talking.

What boosted it all into gear was the Remi remix of "Nappy Heads." After it began getting airplay on the urban contemporary stations, everyone was picking up on it, and the record company decided to make a video of the song. In turn, that was taken on board by MTV, and there was no better way to get the music across to a mass market, a white market. Maybe the Fugees were aiming primarily at their own community, to inform and educate, as well as entertain, but the more power they had in the business, the more likely they were to be heard. And power came from the mass market. If all the suburban kids were going out and buying their records, they'd have money, and money equaled clout. That was important.

And what of Lauryn in all this? A very strange thing happened. In part it was because she was incredibly photogenic—which was just nature, and nothing deliberate on her part—but also because she came across as a strong woman MC in a field where they were few and very far between. She began to be singled out, in press shoots, television interviews, and all manner of things. She wasn't on a trip. "Unfortunately for ladies it's really not that popular in hip-hop to be about much. I'm trying to stand for some things that are strong, black, female and smart, and still fly." To her, this was a band made up of three equal parts. But the press always prefers a pretty face. A few people even began suggesting that she should leave the others behind, that she didn't need them, and that a solo career was the way to go. But she wasn't down with that. "It's not a compliment when people tell me to break off from them," she said. "That's like telling me to drop my brothers. I consider these guys family, so if I act rudely when somebody suggests I go solo, don't think I'm a bitch." And, as Clef added, "The Fugees wasn't pasted together. So it's hard to break us up." Pras was even more certain that they'd be one for all and all for one. "The day that Lauryn [falls off] people will be, like, 'Yo, that bitch is wack,' " he said. "If we split, the force won't be as strong as it was when we were together. So we don't listen to any of that."

Maybe to the media Lauryn was the Fugees, but she and her brothers knew better, and that was all that really mattered. When the sales topped out and the album began sliding back down the charts, the rumors of her going began to circulate again. But the truth was that none of the three was too discouraged by the sales. ''We didn't let the flopness of that first album break us up,'' Pras would say later. ''Lauryn could easily have been like, 'I'm going solo because I can do this by myself . . .' but it's a family. Lauryn didn't let none of that get to her.'' Besides, Wyclef concluded, ''If we took the stuff the critics say seriously, I would have gone back to Haiti.''

Lauryn had completed her first year at Columbia, with a declared major in history. In terms of timing, things had fallen just right. The summer before she became a freshman, she'd had her chance to make another movie, and during the year, *Blunted On Reality* had appeared. There'd been shows, but she'd been able to fit them in without too many demands on her time and her schedule.

Getting into Columbia had been important to her, a vindication not only of her own dreams for a good education, but also those of her parents. She was smart, and no one wanted that to go to waste. Everyone wanted her to make the most of herself in every way. She'd learned a lot, not only about the subject she was studying, but in general. College was a very different atmosphere from high school. She had to impose her own discipline for studying, and much more was expected of her academically in terms of research, papers, and even everyday knowledge. On a daily basis she was mixing with people who talked about ideas. Her precepts were being expanded and questioned constantly. Her mind was stimulated. It was an exciting place. It gave her a buzz.

So, too, did music. Other than her work, it was the love of her life, her chance to be creative and to make her own mark, to offer something to society and to give something back. Her upbringing may have been middle class, but that didn't stop her understanding the struggle of black people in America, of knowing the history, of wanting everything to be right. Teaching was as important as learning, and music gave her the opportunity to teach and be heard.

As summer began, the Fugees were on the road, riding on the back of the success of the "Nappy Heads" remix, playing clubs and wherever they were booked, living in a van for a few weeks, and seeing America as they'd never seen it before. It was an adventure, the kind of thing that would probably have never happened in real life, only in the music business.

After costs, and paying the other musicians in the band, there wasn't a whole lot left over. But it had never been about the money; it was about the *message*. Something they noticed was that the more they played, the tighter they became musically, and the more ideas seemed to both focus and open up. It was an inspiration for all three of them. They were really starting to find themselves, and a unique sound, a true Fugees sound, was beginning to take shape. Clef was bringing in more of the Haitian element and touches of Jamaica that they all loved. Pras was still the rapper, the MC to blow others away on the mic. And Lauryn's singing voice, which had only been heard in snatches on the first record, began to be a vital part of the overall sound, pulling it together, and adding elements of the soul music she'd grown up on in her mother's record collection. As it should, the past constantly informed and helped re-invent the present. As the tour progressed, the Fugees began to get a reputation for smoking shows.

That created a problem and a conflict for Lauryn. At the end of September she was due to begin her sophomore year back in New York City. But there was getting to be more pressure to keep the Fugees on the road, where they were winning an audience that was crossing racial boundaries. Even kids who weren't really into hip-hop were starting to come along, brought in by the musicianship. If she went back to school, all this would be over; they'd be off the road until the following summer, with recording as their only outlet. At the same time, if she quit school, that would be negating everything she'd studied for, and the intellectual progress she'd made in the last twelve months. Columbia was a prestigious school; you didn't turn your back on it to be in a band.

And what would her parents say? The only way to know was to talk it over with them.

They were very supportive. After all, her father had enjoyed his own musical dreams; he understood how she was pulled. What she had to do, they counseled, was what was in her heart. Either way, they would be right behind her.

College, Lauryn reasoned, was something she could go back to. What was happening with the Fugees wouldn't wait forever. This was her shot, her chance to do something with all the music inside her. She wrote to Columbia and asked to be placed on a leave of absence for a year. The college agreed.

four

Roadwork had made the Fugees into a lean, mean music machine. The vision was taking shape, and that meant they were ready, in between stints covering America, to go back into Booga Basement and start sorting out their ideas for what would eventually become a follow-up album. Money was still tight, and Lauryn joked that Clef kept them going by selling off the backing tracks they'd made to other artists. And Wyclef, with a big grin, added that often one client would end up buying the same track—altered just slightly—a second time!

For the Fugees, the basement became their version of Bob Marley's 56 Hope Road, the Tuff Gong Studio where he recorded so much of his amazing material. It was their camp, their place to experiment, to move ahead with what they knew was inside them. As it was *their* studio, they could come and go as they pleased, work all hours without any major thought of the cost. Wyclef wanted to use more acoustic guitar, to have a feeling of spontaneity about it all, and to include more singing; that was a big part of the Fugees show but hadn't been captured on disc. Live, they would happily break into Marvin Gaye's "Sexual Healing," or Marley's "Buffalo Soldier," as well as the old-skool hip-hop of Grandmaster Flash's "White Lines (Don't Do It)," all interspersed with live versions of *Blunted On Reality* material, and new pieces that were still taking shape.

They were all eager to be working, to make the Fugees into what they knew the band could be. But sometimes there were other detours. In 1995, Lauryn added her voice to a track by a couple of other women, Bahamadia and PreCise, "Da Ladies in the House" (Big Kap) which put her back in the spotlight very briefly without the rest of the band.

Mostly, though, she was spending every waking moment with Pras and Clef, and they were working at something that wouldn't sound dated in its production, something that wouldn't sound like anyone else around. This would be dope, and very, very real, said Clef. "We just say keep it realistic. A lot of times you gotta 'shoot' somebody in your lyrics to keep it 'real'—that's not keeping it realistic, because if you shot as many people as you did on your records, you'd be locked up some-where. Whatever you do, it hits you back, so keep preaching positive.'' That was what they'd tried to do on *Blunted On Reality*, some-times with mixed success. This time there would be no compromise. It would be the rec-ord from their heart. And they were in a lucky situation, really. Their debut album might not have performed especially well, but the way people had picked up on the Remi remixes of ''Nappy Heads'' and ''Vocab'' had kept them alive; if anything, it had greatly increased their profile, and had people eager to hear a new record.

One thing the three of them had decided was that this time around, there wouldn't be any outside producer to mess with their music. If anyone knew how the Fugees should sound, it was the Fugees. Not that they weren't proud of the first album, but now they'd truly found a voice. And they knew they were going to be delivering something very special. ''Last time we went copper,'' Pras laughed, ''[this time] I figure we go bronze.'' ''Work our way up through the chain of metals,'' Lauryn com-pleted the joke. Clef wasn't joking about it. He was deadly serious. ''The mass of people, that's what's going to make the Fugees. And the mass you can't stop, because the music we're doing, we're doing for them. Somewhere on this planet, the album will win.''

Those were big claims for something that wasn't even completed yet, but they all had total faith in the project. The way it was coming together, slowly, sometimes painfully, made them all realize that this was going to be something special. ''It's an audio film,'' Lauryn said. ''It's like how radio was back in the forties . . . it tells a story, and there are cuts and breaks in the music. It's almost like a hip-hop version of *Tommy*, like how the Who did for rock'n'roll.'' *Tommy* had been one of the first concept albums, a rock opera as it was called, that had helped make the Who one of the world's biggest rock acts after it was released in 1968. But that was '68, and this was '95. Did the world need another concept record . . . and more to the point, did hip-hop need one at all? What would the concept be, anyway?

There were still forays out from Jersey to play shows, which were just getting better and better, having more in common with the soul greats like James Brown, who made every song into an event, rather than so many of the hip-hoppers, for whom appearing with a crew and just rhyming through the hits was still the order of the day. ''I think the Fugees have made a statement in hip-hop within the last two years,'' Wyclef said, and he was correct. ''At a Fugees show you could expect the next level.'' They delivered, making the music live, mixing up the turntables and the real instruments. Clef would sit at an electric piano or pick up an accordion, L-Boogie on the guitar, Pras hitting a bassline. *That* was making it real. They set a standard for other bands, and challenged them to approach it. But nobody was. Nor were others dragging in reggae and older soul music. For the Fugees, it was all grist to the mill, it was all music that had moved them through their lives, and now it was payback time. And it was all black music; the Fugees were saying it loud and proud.

The record was set for release at the end of January 1996. By Halloween 1995, they'd completed work on it, and given it a title—*The Score*. At that point, the tracks went off to be mastered. The executive producer was Pras, and Lauryn and Clef would be credited as co-executive producers. The first single had already been selected, ''Fu-Gee-La,'' and the band was set to make a video for it during November.

It was too late to rush it out before Christmas, and besides, there would have been no point. It might easily have been lost in the crush of products competing for the seasonal marketplace. In a couple of months, there'd be fewer records coming out, which guaranteed that *The Score*, ''Fu-Gee-La,'' and the Fugees themselves would receive a lot more attention from the media. And it gave them all a break over Christmas. After working so long and so hard, they needed to recharge their own batteries before taking on the world again.

For Lauryn, that meant spending time with her parents in South Orange. This was home. It always had been, and it always would be. Even when she was at Columbia, she'd commuted into New York every day. Home was family and love, being surrounded by the people and things that mattered to her. In a very insecure business, it was a touchstone of security. She could still go up into the attic and look out of the window across to the projects. These days, to a lot of the kids over there, she represented a kind of hope—someone from the 'hood who'd made it, who had a record out, who made a living from music.

As evening fell, she could sit in the little alcove off the dining room with the lights off, and watch the shadows lengthen, just letting the day come to an end. It was a friendly house, as unpretentious as she and her family were, a place of comfort. Christmas brought relatives and friends dropping by, and the house was full on Christmas Day for dinner, with grandparents on both sides arriving. It was also filled with the sound of children, those on the streets around and those from the family running through the house. It held memories, it was part of the fabric that made her who she was. And she had no need to live alone; there was nothing to prove in that. She was often gone, anyway, out on the road. And soon she'd be gone again, when the band headed out to support the new record.

January 31 was the big day. The new year had happened, and winter had the East Coast in its grip. Advances on the record had gone out well before Christmas, and the Fugees had already done a first round of press. Now it was time to wait and see what people thought. One thing was for certain—with *The Score*, listeners wouldn't be getting anything like a standard hip-hop album. "If you want to call us 'alternative,' so be it," Lauryn announced. "We're just trying to bring musicality back to the 'hood."

In March they were on the road, headlining their first big tour around North America, and they were already set to take part in the Smokin' Grooves tour that would run from mid-July to early September. It was a feast of hip-hop and R&B bands all together on one bill—the first time anything like that had happened. Given the violence that tended to explode at some hip-hop shows, it was a daring move, but one that the artists felt would work peaceably.

The Score didn't quite explode out of the box all the way to the top of the charts. Only Pras expected it to sell in huge quantities; the other two didn't care, as long as people got the message. But on the back of "Fu-Gee-La" it all began to take off. It wasn't even a Top Ten single, only climbing to number 29 on the *Billboard* Hot 100, and that took two months. Still, the single sold over half a million copies, enough to claim a gold record, which was more than most singles ever managed. The album moved upward through the *Billboard* chart, going higher and higher, quietly and stealthily. It took thirteen weeks before it topped the album chart, by which time it was already triple platinum, with over three million copies sold.

What had sent it over the top? Why were people buying it like it was going out of style? The answer to that lay in the album's second single. "Killing Me Softly With His Song" was ostensibly a remake of Roberta Flack's 1973 song (which had reached number 1 on its release). Written by Gimble and Fox after seeing him perform, it was about singer/songwriter Don MacLean, the man who made "American Pie" and "Vincent" into radio staples. As the Fugees had envisioned their version of the song, it would have been "Killing Them Softly," not quite a cover, but more of a meditation on the Gs—ghettos, gangsters, and guns—that were killing the black community. Gimble and Fox refused permission for the rewite of their song. But the Fugees loved what they'd done with the piece instrumentally—and so did the record company, who believed it could be a hit—and they decided to do a cover of the original, but in their own style.

Released in May 1996, "Killing Me Softly With His Song" became the tune that summed up the entire year. It was so immediately popular that stores sold out of their stocks of the single, causing a rush at the plants to make more copies. People who wanted it found themselves buying the album just to have it available to hear. It was an automatic number 1 record, and the radio kept playing it (and MTV kept airing the video) all through the summer.

But it wasn't just in America that the Fugees took off like a lightning bolt. In Britain the single *entered* the chart at number 1, which was close to unbelievable, and *The Score* climbed to number 3 there. "It's great, but it doesn't stop here for us," said Pras. "It's like, 'That's cool. You're hot now.' But we've still got work to do, know what I'm saying? It's like we're on a mission." And there was no doubt that the Fugees were the hottest thing in hip-hop—more than that in America. They'd broken out, past the whole idea of "black music" to hot everybody right where they lived. That they'd done it With something as radio-friendly as "Killing Me Softly With His Song" only added to the subversion. Under the sweetness were layers of anger and education. The people were drawn in, and there was plenty of substance to keep them there.

Britain's *New Musical Express* might have written them off derisively as "a covers band," but there was no denying that they were doing exactly what Wyclef had prophesied—they were reaching large numbers of people. How large? Well, the final worldwide sales tally for *The Score* would top seventeen million copies, making it the most successful hip-hop album ever. Putting the musicality back into hip-hop had obviously paid off in a very big way.

"Getting [success] is not hard," Pras said. "Maintaining it, that's the hard thing about it—and keeping your head, and keeping your ego to the level where you can still walk through a door. You've got people whose egos are so big they have to build special houses for them." There was no danger of that happening to any of the Fugees. They might be the darlings of the media, but they were still down with the people. They weren't suddenly living in a rarified world of money. Jersey was home.

Even Clef bought a house there for his parents, over in South Orange, keeping everything very close and familial.

Apart from anything else, there was no chance for them to indulge themselves because the band was back on the road. Having honed their chops out there before, they were eager to get back on the stages. Now, though, instead of poky little places where there was hardly room to move, the demand was enough to have them playing big clubs, and even some small arenas. People wanted the Fugees. Tickets went like hot cakes, and the shows sold out.

The tour started in Canada and worked west. They had opening bands, Goodie Mob and Bahamadia (with whom Lauryn had worked the year before). But it was all about the Fugees, and Clef brought them on with a blast.

"Brooklyn's in the m_____ house! Jersey's in the m_____ house! Haiti's in the m_____ house!", he'd scream in the mic by way of introduction, letting the crowd go wild before the band kicked it. Clef's cousin, Jerry Duplessis, who'd worked with them on the album, was playing bass on the tour, keeping it tight. DJ Leon was behind the decks. At the height of the set as a climax, after playing the guitar with his teeth, Wyclef would turn his back on the audience and then turn back wearing a white hockey mask, shades of Jason and the *Friday the 13th* horror movies. Clef was the musical key, Pras the Master MC, and Lauryn the glue that held it all together, able to switch gears from angry rap to sweet singer without blinking an eyelid. She could do it all.

In the wake of her success with the Fugees, she thought, ''The record companies are gonna jump on the female MC thing right now because it's marketable,'' but she also knew that the labels were going to go more for looks than for acute verbal dexterity, which angered her. ''If you look good, and you rhyme, you get that much more props. If I had one eye lower than the other, I probably wouldn't be as dope as everyone claims I am.'' She thought about what she did, and why she did it. She wasn't in the business to sell sex, or to sell herself, but to have a voice, to do more than just entertain.

''Our whole thing is, we want to show that there's much more to hip-hop than people think,'' commented Clef, and it was obvious that they'd succeeded. They'd managed to cross the boundaries of race, age, and gender to create something with true mass appeal. On a Fugees stage, no one was strutting and grabbing their crotch. It was about musicality. If you needed a true comparison, the best might have been the original Wailers, Bob Marley, Peter Tosh, and Bunny Wailer, who came together and battled the social injustice of their class, of blacks, of the world, through their work in the Wailers. "I'm like a lamb, but I have the fury of a lion," Clef would describe himself. "I'm all about peace and unity and whatever; but I still have the fury of a lion, and I express that lionism through my music."

Later they'd go to Europe, and in London they'd play the Brixton Academy, commemorated in the live version of "Killing Me Softly With His Song" included on the *Bootleg Versions* album, but the band's first North America headlining tour culminated at the beginning of April with a prestige gig at the House of Blues, the club on Sunset. The place was packed with celebrities, including actor Warren Beatty, who'd never been known as a big fan of hip-hop. He'd come down not just to check the show—the word was out about just how hot the Fugees were live—but to see Lauryn on the stage. "She's just a kid," he said afterward, "but she's an old soul with uncommon humility, beauty, and musicality. She's totally devoid of bull----." And she was all that and more. She was a fighter for human rights, for her community, and above all, for the band she loved, that people had tried to rip apart before. "That's my family," she told everyone, "those are my people. We've been together since I was thirteen, and I love the music we make.''

But even then, she was looking ahead and telling reporters that one day she'd probably release a solo record, doing it on her own terms. According to what she was saying then, the Fugees were talking to Columbia, the label that distributed Ruffhouse, about having their own label called ''Refugee Camp Records''; their production company was called Refugee Camp Entertainment. ''This way,'' she pointed out, ''we'll be the ones exploiting ourselves.''

Throughout the spring and summer, and long into the fall, *The Score* continued to sell all over the world, and in one unguarded moment, Lauryn supposedly caused a bit of controversy. Reportedly, on Howard Stern's radio show, she said that the Fugees wrote for their own community, the people who'd grown up the way they had, and that the success of *The Score* hadn't made them into sellouts. In fact, she'd have been just as happy selling fewer records, if it meant that more blacks had bought them.

This generated criticism that she didn't want to sell records to white people and that she was racist. She felt badly misrepresented. Racism was one thing she was against, in any shape or form, and would never have condoned. Of course she wanted to sell records, but she was black herself, and she was writing about the things that were real in her black life and in all black lives. She wanted to communicate those to her brothers and her sisters—her own community. For them to listen and to be educated was her prime goal, and the goal of all the Fugees. She told the truth, and if people wanted to manufacture a controversy where none actually existed, that was out of her hands. The simple fact was that the Fugees were huge, and they were in the public eye. They didn't indulge in wild parties—they didn't need to or want to—and there were no scandals to report about the group. So things were invented, or some creative spin put on them to be sensational. The band themselves wanted unity, peace—and that meant *all* people.

Success was fine, but it hadn't brought real happiness. For a while, Lauryn had been head over heels in love with a man, and when it ended, she had to cope with her heartbreak on the road. The work might have given her the chance to focus on something else, but only postponed the grieving and made it worse. ''I'm a lot hurt and I'm a lot disappointed,'' she said. ''Half of the niggas that I meet, they don't know about relationships. And when they hurt you, they don't know about it. Or if they do know, they don't really give a f_____ because they've been so bruised, battered and scarred themselves.'' It was a mix of bitterness and extreme pain talking. They'd been together quite a while, and Lauryn had believed that it could last forever. Coming off the tour, there should have been time for herself and to give herself a chance to assimilate the situation. Instead she threw herself into more work, rather than have the free time to reflect and think. If she was busy, she could focus on something else.

She knew just how hot the band was, and she also knew that she wanted to be able to give something back to the black communities, to those who hadn't had the breaks. It was a responsibility thing, and it was important to her, to all of them. They'd made a lot of money, and they had power in the industry; and it was time to use both to help others.

Lauryn's first act was to organize a free concert in Harlem. Not only would it give the kids—and the adults—a chance to see some top hip-hop names without having to pay, but the drive at the back of it was to increase voter registration. If you didn't vote, you couldn't change the system. And it was the system that had helped create an underclass.

She did it all with the help of Suzette Williams, who'd shortly be working with Lauryn. People said it was an impossible task, bringing together a lot of acts, many of whom were real prima donnas. The first thing they needed was money, and Lauryn herself called executives at record companies, asking for donations. In less than a month, she accumulated almost $200,000 for the show and had promises of performances from some of the biggest names. It was called "Hoodshock," a play on Woodstock, of course, and more than 10,000 people turned up to see Wu-Tang Clan, the Notorious B.I.G., who would sadly die the following year, and Sean "Puffy" Combs perform in May 1996, at one of the biggest shows Harlem had ever seen.

The organizing lit a fire under Lauryn and made her want to do more, which led to the foundation of the Refugee Project. A concert had been one thing, offering entertainment to those who often couldn't afford the ticket prices at a real show, but she wanted something that would help others more directly, particularly the young. Suzette Williams became the treasurer of the project, which is still very much in existence and alive.

The Refugee Project was designed to reach out into communities, and in some cases, to offer seed money and assistance for things that would enrich the community and help people to help themselves. It supported well-building projects for villages in Kenya and Uganda, and at home, the Project sponsored day camps for inner-city kids from Newark and other places in New Jersey. Lauryn wasn't about to let anyone tell her she couldn't do these things; she went ahead and did them. "She takes an idea and makes it happen," said Suzette Williams. "She's not scared of obstacles, she's not scared of opposition, and that's rare." For Lauryn, the Project and the works it undertook, became, and still is, an important part of her everyday life. She was making far more money than she'd ever dreamed and than she could ever use. It was only right to give some of it back to help others.

She did allow herself one indulgence with her new wealth, though—she bought a house. Oddly enough, it wasn't for herself, but for her parents, a bigger place than the one they now owned but just a couple of blocks away. The deal was this: Lauryn would continue to live in what had been the family house, and her parents would move to the new, roomier one. Totally unpretentious, Lauryn didn't need a mansion, or a Rolex on her wrist, or gold chains on her neck to show she was worth something as a person; she already knew her own value. She loved the house, and wanted to live there.

Between one thing and another, there was very little free time for Lauryn in the month the Fugees had off. There was the business of the Project, buying the house for her parents, and she managed to squeeze a few hours to record with rapper Nas, adding her voice to one of his tracks, "It Was Written," as well as background vocals on Set It Off's "Set It Off." At the beginning of July, it was time to hit the road with the Smokin' Grooves tour.

In between, the band had turned down a very lucrative offer to make a commercial for Sprite with basketball superstar Penny Hardaway. And it made sense; it would have devalued the ideals they were trying to have put across, selling them for pennies on the dollar. "We're number one on the charts, and black people haven't had anything like us in a while," Clef said. "But we feel like we stand for something more. This group's saying something about police brutality, the government, social issues, and straight-up hip-hop." To have taken Madison Avenue's money would have been to lose all credibility, another act gone over to the corporate machine. As it was, the Fugees might have been working within the system, but they were outside the system, subversive.

Smokin' Grooves had been planned as a kind of hip-hop version of Lollapalooza, a show that traveled around the country, staging one-day shows in a number of locations. It began on July 22, 1996 in Sacramento, California, and ended on September 2, at the begininng of the Labor Day weekend, in Devore, California. Their multi-platinum status ensured that the Fugees would have a headlining slot. It was more gigs, more time on the road, and another six weeks without a break. One thing Lauryn had no way of knowing was that it would change her life completely.

Bob Marley, who was born in Jamaica in 1945 and died of cancer in 1981, was a true legend. He'd started recording in the 1960s in Kingston, and with his friends Peter Tosh and Neville Livingstone (who would rename himself Bunny Wailer), formed the Wailers, one of the hottest groups of the ska era in Jamaica. They stayed together and grew musically, working with producer Lee Perry in the late 1960s, and at the start of the next decade, now a full band, moved to London where they eventually signed a record contract with Island Records. Their first two albums, *Catch A Fire* and *Burnin'* established them as the foremost band in reggae, playing songs that were both catchy and deep. After that, Tosh and Wailer left the band, which was then renamed Bob Marley and the Wailers, and over the course of the 1970s, Marley became an international figure, a songwriter who spoke out against repression in some wonderful songs, and who also put on incredible live shows. In Jamaica, his fame made him a national hero, especially after a

1976 assassination attempt. He became one of the world's best known, and most respected, black men.

He fathered a number of children, some of whom, under the leadership of his son Ziggy, formed the Melody Makers and went on to international fame in their own right. After Marley was diagnosed with cancer, he ended up in Miami, where his mother, Cedella Booker, now lived, and he passed away in a hospital there.

Marley's son, Rohan, born in 1972, had spent some of his time growing up in Miami with his grandmother, who had become his adoptive parent on his father's death. He resembled his father, but where Bob had been wiry, Rohan was stocky, solid and muscular. Bob had been a gifted soccer player (who liked to often play in bare feet, as he had done when a child), and Rohan inherited his father's athletic skills. He became a football player, and would end up playing for the University of Miami. Like his dad, he wore his hair in the standard Rastafarian style of dreadlocks. Unlike many of his siblings, Rohan wasn't musical, so the place at the University of Miami also gave him the chance to get a degree.

While he didn't play any instruments, a love of music was definitely in his genes, and hip-hop as much as reggae had been part of the soundtrack of his adolescence. He still loved it, and when the Smokin' Grooves tour hit Miami, he was there to check everyone out, especially the Fugees, who had covered his father's classic song, "No Woman, No Cry" on *The Score*. Being a Marley opened a lot of doors in the music business—and they meant all-access backstage passes for Rohan Marley. That was how he met Lauryn Hill.

"He said, 'Hey,'" she recalled, " 'Hey, I like you. I want to talk to you.' But back then I wasn't really checking for anybody. I was very much into my music. You know, I'd spent so many years working a relationship that didn't work that I was just like, 'I'm going to write these songs and pour my heart into them.'" Rohan, though, was very much checking for her, and wasn't about to be put off so easily. He persisted, showing up at gigs, talking to her, and it wasn't long before they began dating. Their interests were similar. The same things made them laugh and made them cry. Lauryn was still carrying around a weight of unhappiness, but it lifted a little when she was around Rohan. "Rohan was the first guy I was with who actually took care of me. He protects me like a lion." As the two drew closer, her life seemed to be on an even keel again. She could even begin to enjoy the success that was happening to the band.

five

The *Score* had turned the world upside down for the Fugees, and made them conquerors, going where no hip-hop album had gone before. To sell seventeen million copies of *any* album was an incredible achievement. For a hip-hop record, it was completely unprecedented. But then, there'd never been a hip-hop record like this before.

It was the product of three minds with the same goal, working furiously and in complete harmony. And in many ways it was like a movie, as Lauryn had said, stories unfolding, snippets of dialogue. To listen to the way it was put together did give a deeper understanding of *Blunted On Reality*, as Pras had predicted. But where that was sometimes pedestrian, this was totally original, a mix of R&B, hip-hop, pop, and even soul, all with that definite groove of music coming from the heart. They weren't afraid to check the names of those who'd influenced them, and also to pay home to the old skool of rap by using the talents of DJ Red Alert on the into and the outro tracks. It connected it all and placed the record in a continuum of history.

"Intro" set the scene, a gangsta scene, but one which didn't praise the gangsta ethic. Instead "Intro" dissed it, finding the power in a family, a business, something positive. But as the man said, you had to be a soldier.

It bled into "How Many Mics," which was hip-hop, but nowhere near as hard as the tracks that had appeared on the Fugees first album. It put down the old style—the gangsta style— that had become so old and tired. And it did it over the beats and a spooky keyboard line from Clef, with Lauryn letting it rip, before the chorus, which mixed rap with Lauryn's sung background—totally different from anything else around. She handed off to Clef, who said his part about the way violence was glorified, and then it was Pras's turn. While the track was superficially about violence, it was very much anti-violence, and full of mad asides (like Clef's quote from the old hit "I Wear My Sunglasses at Night") which were just pure stream of consciousness studio inspiration. This was hip-hop on a completely new level, laid back, a far cry from the Public Enemy cop that had been their previous approach—and all the more powerful for it.

Then came the dialogue, acting like a Greek chorus to move the action along. It introduced the panning keyboard chords of "Ready or Not," which sampled "Ready or Not, Here I Come (Can't Hide from Love)," which had been a 1969 hit for the soul group, the Delfonics. They used it as the basis of a song—sweet on the surface, coating the bitterness and anger inside—against America's stated policy to those who came seeking asylum. The song also used a sample from "Boadecia," by New Age artist Enya, which had appeared on her album *The Celts*. Initial copies of the album didn't give attribution because the sample had been used without permission. A settlement was reached, and future copies of the CD booklet thanked Enya for her "kindness and consideration" in allowing the sample to be used. "Ready or Not," which was one of the hit singles the album produced, was readily familiar on the airwaves, in part for the new direction it took the Fugees, with Lauryn's glorious singing voice getting free rein on record for the first time. It led into and worked under Clef's rap, the way so many lived in poverty, and the allure was the very sparseness of the sound, the way Lauryn's voice overdubbed and wove around itself before sliding into her rhymes, a rant against all the gangstas. Then it was Lauryn's sung bridge, then Pras on the mic. The Fugees tick of sliding things in, odd bits of speech, encouragement, and lyrics, worked to utter perfection here.

"Zealots," took off with a sample of "I Only Have Eyes for You" as the springboard, and the sense of being watched. (There was even a reference to Rockwell, whose "Somebody's Watching Me" had been a hit and an MTV favorite in the eighties—but the band was very strong on throwing in all sorts of pop culture references.) Lauryn's middle section, sung and spoken, was nothing less than stunning, leading into her own rhyme—and a namecheck to Carlos Santana, probably never dreaming she'd work with him in a couple of years—where she was happy to diss the cursing that so many rappers seemed to think was mandatory in order to be heard and taken as serious and tough. Clef's chorus, while using the melody of "I Only Have Eyes for You," brought in a reggae feeling, an unusual blend of doo-wop and Jamaica—but it worked—before criticizing those who said Lauryn should go solo. This was a manifesto—the Fugees were back and stronger than ever!

It was the *way* they worked that was innovative, the fact that they could subvert the sweet to their own ends, juxtaposing it against the grim reality of black life. And their positive vibration was something quite different from anything else around. Arrested Development had offered something slightly similar a few years before, giving a rural feeling to hip-hop, but that had proven to be something of a dead end, as had the jazzy tip of Digable Planets more recently. Although both had influenced the course of the music, they hadn't been able to sustain their own progress. The Fugees were taking all of that and adding their own original and decidedly political vision. The track ended with the voices of the chorus discussing how the police sometimes treated blacks before mutating into the next cut, ''The Beast.''

No samples this time around, just the band playing. ''The Beast'' was authority of all sorts—the government, and most particularly, the police and prison, a place where many blacks end up. Backspin was responsible for the scratching behind it all, as Pras spun his tale of being pulled over by the police in New Jersey, an event that brought the fate of Rodney King into his mind—as it inevitably could. What should he do, pull over or just take off? It was a thought that probably came into the minds of many young black men in similar situations, real food for thought, and another brutally honest slice of daily life, an illumination of the problems of life for the black race.

Then the chorus returned, going for Chinese food and being mistreated by the restaurant owner, part of the continual clashes between the races—not just white and black, but all races.

From there, "Fu-Gee-La" took off. It had been the album's first hit single, the warning cry that the Fugees were back and in full effect. Taking a sample from Tina Marie's 1985 hit, "Ooh La La La," it was a statement of where the band stood and what affected them, a political stance that also reworked the older song to superb ends. They were decidedly returning the soul to hip-hop, which had almost disappeared since the old skool were sampling the beats from James Brown's "Funky Drummer." This was the Refugee ethic that was behind everything they did, the journey we are all on, in one form or another. Dogma of any kind—religion, capitalism, anything—was dangerous. They could make you think, rock your world, and get your booty on the dance floor as well. It was where everything came together, mixing, for want of better terms, pop and politics, and proving that they didn't need to be strange bedfellows. In many respects, this was the record's centerpiece, its true statement of purpose, both musically and lyrically. By combining all the elements that made the album so special—Lauryn's singing, the conscious rhymes, and the judicious and thoughtful, sparing use of samples—the Fugees created something that was intoxicatingly fresh and original. They were reborn with this track and this album. The sense of purpose had always been there, but now they were saying it *their* way.

The chorus of voices again served as the introduction to "Family Business." Family meant many things. Clef's guitar played a Haitian rhythm behind the rhymes about the black state of the union, with guest appearances by Forte and Omega. Family could be those who'd raised you, those who you were related to by blood, or the family of the streets—and within families there could be feuds. And if people were driven to crime, sometimes it was the state that was responsible. Even the streets were unsafe in areas—there was no secret there—as the evil armies took over the projects and the corners after dark. It became a meditation on the possibilities of sudden death—another fact of everyday life for someone growing up in the ghetto.

The chorus made it clear that "Killing Me Softly With His Song" had a meaning that went beyond the obvious meaning of the song's original lyrics, and Lauryn too announced that, before the song truly began, over Clef's voice that was dubbed out with echo.

Then, with a church-like grace, Lauryn began singing. Lauryn had been responsible for the arrangement and the backing vocals. She took off singing just over a funky beat, soulful as Aretha, then let the bass in to add its resonance as she built up a gospel choir of overdubs, taking the song somewhere it had never gone before. It didn't need a big orchestration; there was enough melody in the song as it stood, and Lauryn's voice was all the embellishment it really needed. This was her moment in the singing spotlight, not a diva, but someone steeped in the soul tradition whose close roots were the church. It was delicate and beautiful, but the bass and drums kept it grounded on the floor, and it was an undeniable hit.

The title track of *The Score* was about people who talk loud and a lot, but say nothing. There were scores to be settled, and Clef could do it with his words. Diamond D, from Diggin in Da Crates, guested, but this was the Fugees gig. It brought in bits from other tracks, almost an overture inserted halfway through the music, and a reaffirmation of the fact that the Fugees weren't about to back down from their position for anything. The other MCs might try to be intimidating, but their words were empty. The Fugees had meaning because they had the spirit behind them moving and propelling them along. They were soldiers, but their battle wasn't with other gangs; it was with those who'd try to be the negative forces in life, whether on the streets, in the precinct houses, or in the Senate. There comes a time when everyone has to be willing to stand up and be counted for what they believe, and the band was standing loud and very proud, and completely unafraid because God and right were on their side. They would blow the other MCs away—verbally only, of course.

"The Mask" used a strange little xylophone line to bring in the voices. It was about the masks we have to wear, about being someone we really aren't, including Clef's reminiscences of working at a fast food restaurant and being offered a quarter raise to inform on the other employees. And it was about people fronting, like the guy who tried to hit on Lauryn. Musically this was the most adventurous of the tracks—bringing in jazz influences, very noir-ish, namechecking the Notorious B.I.G., a snaky saxophone line winding through it all. Eventually, of course, the masks come down . . . for everyone.

"Cowboys," with guest appearances from Pace 1, Young Zee, and Ra Digga, was about the way America has glorified the image of the cowboy, the cult of the gun, of taking what you want by force. The West was won by the gun, and it was the enforcer of the ghetto. The criminals of the West became its folk heros, and in the ghetto the criminals were the folk legends—the comparisons of lawlessness were obvious. With suitable spaghetti western guitar in the background, ominous chords and a simple beat, they laid it out—even down to the country and western yodels. Even a quote from Kenny Rogers's "The Gambler" was used, as was John Wayne and the old "Cowboys to Girls" soul classic. Was the ghetto new West? No, of course not, and by mythologizing it, no one was being done any favors. The cycle of violence was merely continued.

The song cycle, the movie, reached its climax with another cover song, this time Bob Marley's "No Woman, No Cry," dedicated by Clef to all the refugees around the world. Change the locale from Trenchtown in Jamaica to Brooklyn in New York, and the song was still completely applicable, as the man sang over his acoustic guitar (instead of the churchy organ of the original). It was a classic song, and utterly relevant, with lyrics only slightly updated. Lauryn did a wonderful job on the backing vocals, sounding for all the world like Marley's backing trio, the I-Threes. It was a low-key way to end things, quite sobering, but at the same time, uplifting, as Marley had intended. No more needed to be said, really. Keeping it so spare, just the voices, programmed drums, bass, and acoustic guitar, kept it intimate and real, the way the Fugees themselves were. In comparison to their debut, this was stripped-down.

Then it came to an end with "Manifest/ Outro," scratching by DJ Scribble. This was a parable of good people being betrayed by evil, as Jesus was by Judas, a situation that continues every day—drug addicts, violence, you name it. We all needed to get past that before we could move on as a race.

After that, it was on to what were essentially the bonus cuts, although only one of them was marked that way. "Fu-Gee-La (Refugee Camp Mix)" was essentially Wyclef's vision of the track, which had been produced for the album by Salaam Remi, the man who'd helped break them his remixes of "Nappy Heads" and "Vocab." It was even more laid back than the original, something that offered a slightly Caribbean vibe. There were even a few dub effects applied, with the other instruments cutting out, leaving just the drums behind Clef's voice. That sensibility would be even more apparent on the other remix of the track that appeared next, by reggae legends Sly and Robbie. Sly Dunbar and Robbie Shakespeare were one of reggae's great rhythm sections, playing drums and bass respectively, and they'd helped bring Jamaican music forward into the real electronic age. (Sly played both acoustic and electric drum kits.) But they'd also established themselves as producers, working with acts on their own Taxi label and others. Here Sly played regular drums and was responsible for the drum programming, with Robbie on the bass, Handel Tucker on keys, and toasting—the early Jamaican style of rap— by Garfield "Gus" Parkinson of the Stone Love Crew. The track had been recorded at Anchor Studios in Kingston, Jamaica, with Tucker producing and handling the mix along with engineer Eddie Hudson.

This was much more hardcore reggae, with Robbie's unmistakable bass work under the rhymes, showing just how influenced by reggae the track was. Plenty of dub effects of delay and echo contributed to the spaciness of it, and Parkinson's toasting connected it all. Even more than covering Bob Marley, this established the Fugees' reggae credentials as very much the real thing, and better than a lot of the music that had come out of Jamaica for a few years, where so much had been dancehall style and "slackness" or sexual innuendo. One of the few Jamaican artists with uplifting, "conscious" lyrics was Buju Banton (along with Bounty Killa), and some of his influence was in this remix. Even Lauryn's singing seemed to have more in common with her sisters in Jamaica than New Jersey. It stood both as a remix and a completely different creation, as every good remix should, with the personality of the remixers intertwining with the original artists to create something new, without losing the spirit of the original.

The final cut, and the real bonus, was "Mista Mista," which was Wyclef and his acoustic guitar, showing that he also had a remarkable singing voice, with a wide range. And his song of the disenfranchised, raising a lot of questions, was a very strong social anthem, and an indication that he was actually a very sophisticated writer of songs, including straight songs. To be fair, it didn't sit in with the rest of the album, but it was too good not to be included here—a superb, provocative way to close things out. There were no easy answers, but that didn't mean the questions should remain unasked. Someone had to be brave enough to open his mouth.

So just what had Lauryn, Pras, and Clef created with *The Score*? It sprawled at times; it was ambitious. But it worked, this strange mix of styles, times, and cultures, to create a unity that couldn't be denied. It was compelling, even for someone who wasn't into hip-hop. In fact it was the perfect album for someone who wasn't into hip-hop, since that was only one piece of the whole. As an album about unity, it melded the influences of old skool rap, of nineties hip-hop, of reggae, of Haiti—all with a lot of soul. When they used their samples, they became an integral part of the song, in some cases being the focal point, which meant they were almost reworking the originals. With covers of "Killing Me Softly With His Song" and "No Woman, No Cry," it did mean that the Fugees were a covers band. But only to a certain extent. Whatever they did was so strongly imbued with their own personalities that they couldn't help but make the songs their own. And those familiar tunes did serve as an introduction for a whole new audience, many of whom had probably never bought a hip-hop album before.

They'd re-emerged stronger and more individual than ever. Their success changed the entire course of hip-hop and of music. If someone wanted to be derisive and simply call them a covers band, that was fine; they knew exactly who and what they were. "Whatever they're saying, it doesn't affect us," Clef said. "We the ones that gotta walk on Flatbush [Avenue]." They talked the talk, and they were strong enough to walk the walk. They'd kept it real, and that was all that mattered. Still that didn't mean they couldn't have their own particular favorite songs. " 'Ready or Not' is my favorite song on the album," Pras commented.

"The day we did that song, the three of us was each going through some pain. L was crying when she did her vocals. It was unbelievable. To see her singing with tears coming out of her eyes, it made me want to cry too." What had been singing to mark the bittersweet, painful end of a relationship had turned into a tune of victory through 1996. On the Smokin' Grooves tour it had been an important song, one to show that the Fugees sound had truly won as the crowds roared for them at every stop.

By now Rohan Marley had become an almost constant companion of Lauryn. He was there backstage at the shows and would leave with her later. And she was a changed person from the sad woman who'd been around early in the year. If it wasn't love, it was something very close, and was definitely developing that way. She was with him for who he was, not because of his name and all that signified. It was the man she cared about, not the myth behind his surname. And it was obvious that he cared equally for her, and that the two of them seemed *right* together.

Even after Smokin' Grooves, and a straight six months on the road, there was no end in sight for the band. The demand was so high that they had to take off for Europe once again. And there was a new version of "No Woman,

No Cry'' to be cut, with another of Bob's sons, Stephen Marley, singing with Clef, while Lauryn and Sharon Marley (a Marley daughter) contributed to the backing vocals, with some heavy hitters from the reggae world, including Earl "Chinna" Smith, providing the instrumentation.

That was a single in Britain, the video was shot at the recording session, and it became another hit. In America, it would appear on the *Bootleg Versions* EP, a veritable jumble of Fugees odds and ends that was rushed out by the record label to capitalize on the demand for Fugees product in the wake of *The Score*'s phenomenal and continuing success.

The Fugees in New York City, 1996.
(Susan Stava/Retna Ltd.)

Lauryn takes the mic. (Drew Farrell/Retna Ltd.)

Reaching out to the people in Haiti.
(Youri Lenquette/@priori)

Lauryn sports her trademark bangles.
(Youri Lenquette/Retna Ltd.)

The Fugees at the 1996 MTV Video Music Awards. (Larry Busacca/Retna Ltd.)

Lauryn kicks it on stage
(Youri Lenquette/Retna Ltd.)

At the 1998 Billboard Music Awards.
(Steve Granitz/Retna Ltd.)

six

In a way, it made perfect sense to gather up the odds and ends, stray tracks and remixes into one package, and it was done in a way that didn't offer any disservice to the band. And there was no denying that they were hot. As platinum followed platinum on the album, people genuinely did want to hear more, and there were no other new tracks laid down, nor did the band have the time to go into the studio to work on anything to their own satisfaction.

It kicked in with "Ready or Not (Clark Kent/Django Remix)" with extra contributions from Clef and Red Alert. It utilized a very interesting sample, "Django," written by John Lewis and performed by the Modern Jazz Quartet, which naturally gave a completely different flava to the song. It was radically different, bringing out even more Lauryn's singing. The two elements mixed perfectly, the smoky jazz sounds mingling with soul and hip-hop to create a continuity of black consciousness.

"Nappy Heads (Mad Spider Mix)" was totally different from the version that had appeared on *Blunted by Reality*, with Clef's Jamaican style very much to the fore. It was produced by Clef and Pras, and with its references, curious as it might sound, was one of Clef's favorite ways of relaxing. A trumpet offered the only musical color, a faint texture in the relentless ragga. Did it all work? Yes, but after a little while, it was just too hardcore for any casual listener. By isolating only one bit of the original, it did create an accent.

"Don't Cry Dry Your Eyes" was a Fugees tune that hadn't appeared anywhere before, and sounded as though it were taken from *The Score* sessions, but it was actually recorded in London, at Air Studios. Produced by Wyclef and Jerry Duplessis and co-produced by Lauryn, this was just cool modern hip-hop. Lauryn's rhymes cut over the guitar like a knife before Pras handled the mic. This was the way they could do it live, this was creativity, the cutting edge of hip-hop. Everyone had their contribution, with L's singing coming behind it all.

"Vocab (Salaam's Remix)" had never been available on an album before, and as an important part of the band's history, it needed to be there. It had kept the flame alive, and made it burn even hotter between *Blunted on Reality* and *The Score*. It added a beat, some backgrounds, and made a wonderful track even more enduring.

Remi was also responsible for the next cut, his remix of "Ready or Not." It was only right to give him a crack at the song, with all he'd done for the band. This brought more of a Jamaican flava, something that was coming in more and more to the Fugees music, by using a sample from Jamaican singer Barrington Levy's "Here I Come." By changing the instrumental backing to something a bit less defined, it altered the whole mood of the song, even though the rhymes themselves remained the same.

"Killing Me Softly With His Song" showed another, equally valid side of the Fugees—the live show. Captured at Brixton Academy, there was a very appealing rawness to it. No rich backing vocals this time, but a rhythm section and Clef and the piano, with lots of vocal exhortations by both Clef and Pras. It really showcased Lauryn's exquisite voice, which could go from silky smooth to soul roughness within a single beat. It was short, but somehow that didn't matter. It was just the song, and nothing more, stripped down and soulful.

The remix of "No Woman, No Cry" owed

much more to the Marley version than the one the Fugees had released on *The Score*. Stephen Marley's voice was an eerie echo of his father's, maybe not quite as rich, but close enough to make someone listen very closely. Lauryn, Sharon Marley, Eric Newell, and Pamela Hall did a wonderful approximation of the I-Threes, and the simulated crowd noise at the end of the first line made it obvious that the immediate inspiration for this was the version Marley had recorded in 1975 on his *Live* album. Taro McLaughlin's organ was suitably churchy, and as the song speeded up, it truly did sound as though everything was going to be all right. Clef certainly had never sounded more soulful. This was homage to a master and to some of the band's roots. It was also apparent that Clef had developed into an exceptional producer. And the vibe, Clef insisted, was that when they sat down to mix the song, right after recording it, the power went out in the studio (and for six blocks around), as if it was just a sign that they shouldn't do it then and there.

"Vocab (Refugees Hip-Hop Mix)", produced by Clef and Pras, took the song in a totally different direction, keeping only the guitar figure and the refrain, while Pras and L took the mics and told some of the history of the crew, how they'd come to hip-hop, and the things that had moved them along the way.

All in all, *Bootleg Versions* was a valuable addition to the Fugees recorded canon. Nothing wasted, no garbage, just plenty more good music. There were almost forty minutes of it—anything under forty minutes was officially classed as an EP, not an album.

Another valuable addition was the release of a long form video, *The Score . . . Bootleg Versions*, which included a lot of interview footage with the band, both in a park and in their sanctuary of the Booga Basement (which turned out to be, quite literally, the basement of a house, perhaps an odd place to be the headquarters of one of the world's biggest bands). They talked about the formation of the band, but the real reason people bought it was for the videos included, all that the band had done in their career, from "Boof Baf" off *Blunted On Reality* to "No Woman No Cry." It really showed how much the band had developed, and how much more sophisticated they'd become at using video to get their message across. Produced and directed by Marc Smerling, it made for a very interesting package indeed.

The video for "Boof Baf" was every bit as raw as the music itself. Made mostly in black and white, with just some flashes of color, there was no real story to it, just the flashing images of the band, of people working like slaves, then hearing the word read from the good book. Filmed on some derelict prperty that almost looked like it could have been in the Caribbean, but which was actually either Brooklyn or the Bronx, it did at least help signify the way blacks had been used and oppressed, with their only freedoms in religion and dancing.

Next came the two songs that had helped raise the Fugees standard before *The Score*, the remixes of "Vocab" and "Nappy Heads." "Vocab" was very much a street video, again mostly black and white, shot in the projects. Wyclef played the very distinctive guitar part on his worn acoustic, as both Lauryn and Pras celebrated the Fugees and hip-hop. Again, it was raw and quite cheaply made. But at that point they were a band still struggling, without the luxury of a big budget with which to promote themselves. Much the same rang true for "Nappy Heads," which was largely in a sepia tone. Lauryn filmed her part at her stomping grounds, outside the library at Columbia University in New York where she'd been a student, and Clef was shown both outside a barber shop, and then inside, getting his head shaved clean. When the crew got together, it was on a cobble street, where a jazz rhythm section provided backing, and the band hung out with their crew—which was what the music was all about. Once more, it was a cheap video to make, more out of necessity than any artistic statement. But it had received plenty of airplay, and kept expectations high for *The Score*, which had more than delivered.

For the videos for the tracks from *The Score*, the band had a real budget to work with, and they used every penny of it. Lauryn had referred to the album as an audio film; this gave them the chance to add the visuals and they did that in fine style, filming in Jamaica. It wasn't exactly a vacation, though, but plenty of long, long days and hard work. The band did all their own stunts for the video, which would be divided into three parts, for "Fu-Gee-La," "Ready Or Not," and then "Killing Me Softly With His Song," which would tie it all together.

"Fu-Gee-La" was the start of the story, with the Fugees as agents, stealing a bribe that had been made to a high official. Pras and Clef came by on a moped and snatched the briefcase off the sidewalk as the official sat in a café. Lauyrn was suspected and stopped by police. She made her getaway and joined the others escaping in a pickup truck, with the police in hot pursuit. They crashed a roadblock, but when the cops killed the driver, the Fugees took to the jungle, jumping down a waterfall in an attempt to stay free. At an abandoned house they managed to evade their followers, hightailing it down to the harbor, where they could catch the ferry and leave the island. But they were a few moments too late. The ferry had gone, and the police were waiting. Lauryn did what she could. She opened the case, dumping the money onto the dock, and while the cops were going for it, the trio jumped into the water (which wasn't great for Clef, who couldn't swim).

Part Two came with "Ready or Not," which took three grueling days to film. This was big-time expense, opening as it did with a fleet of helicopters after Pras, who was on his jetski. He had a mission, to free the refugee Clef, who'd been caught and was in prison, beaten by the guards. He managed to do it, and the two of them, plus a waiting Lauryn, vanished on motorcycles, as the helicopters came hot on their trail. But they had a secret weapon, quite literally, that the military didn't know about. Just offshore they had a submarine. They dove off a pier (again!), and Pras located the sub, bringing it to the surface, so Lauryn and Clef could board it. They were ready to free the island, by force if necessary, but it wasn't the whole story. That would be rounded off with the third episode, "Killing Me Softly With His Song."

That took place in a movie theater. As the crowds outside waited to get in, the Fugees emerged from their limo and scampered inside, beneath a sign announcing that night's feature "The Fugees—The Score." As bits of the other two videos played onscreen, with Lauryn singing along to the track, the life of a theater carried on around them. The audience got into the film. There were popcorn fights. Girls flirted with boys and led them on. It was, Lauryn said, a very deliberate attempt to get the old-skool, *Cooley High*-type of vibe, one which was very true to real life. But more than that, Clef explained, it made you realize that the other two parts had just been a movie, and there were the Fugees watching it all onscreen. It made them less like stars, and more a part of the audience, which was exactly what they wanted, to indicate that there was actually very little difference between them and their audience. They were real, and they were human, not superstars but genuine people. The video was as good as the song, and MTV loved it enough to give it an award as R&B Video of the year, although, given its success as a single, it had transcended any kind of genre. It simply was.

"Cowboy" kept to the same movie theater theme, and in fact, the same movie theater. This time what else could they be watching but a Western? As the wanted posters for all of the band members appeared on the screen, the audience in the theater began watching the film, with its spaghetti western guitar line. Clef was the wild man, the Clint Eastwood figure in his poncho. Lauryn was the fly girl, not dressed for a Western, but who really cared? And Pras rode right into the saloon on the back of a house, before getting involved in a card game. The shot moved back and forth between the theater—where the crowd was loving every minute of it—and the screen, finishing off with the Fugees riding out of town, and vanishing into the sunset, like all Western heroes.

Then it all rounded off with the great vibe of "No Woman No Cry," which had everything to do with family, sitting around the studio and actually recording the track, and was a wonderful note on which to end it all.

By the end of 1996, the band was exhausted. It had been a long, and a very major effort from them. They moved up from just another band playing hip-hop to *the* band in the world. There was an MTV Video Music Award for R&B video of the year, for "Killing Me Softly With His Song," and it seemed very likely there'd be some Grammy nominations coming in January. Nineteen ninety-seven promised a lot more.

For Lauryn, though, the end of 1996 marked a turning point in her personal life. She discovered that she was pregnant. It hadn't been planned, but it left her with a great deal of soul-searching to do. When she announced the fact, there was immediate speculation as to who might be the father—one thing she deliberately didn't tell to the media. Her relationship with Rohan was private. They didn't hang out in the public places, at the clubs and parties. Some suggested that Wyclef was responsible. Lauryn kept her mouth shut. There were much bigger issues going on.

The biggest question of all was, should she keep the baby?

"A lot of people said, 'Girl, you've got a career. Don't be having no baby now.'" And it was true. The Fugees were incredibly successful, and they could only get bigger. Being pregnant, with all its stresses and strains, didn't mix well with life on the road, and there was pressure on the band to keep touring. Finally she decided to look into her heart to see what she should do. "I looked at myself in the mirror and I said, 'Okay, now this is a hard one,' and I prayed on it. What I do know is that God is never going to give you a sign to not have a child if you are pregnant. That sign will never come. At least it didn't for me. In my brain I said, 'I'm okay financially. I have a man in my life who loves me. I have a supportive family. I believe I would be a good mother.' I said, 'Wow, the only reason for me not to have this child is because it would inconvenience me.'

And that wasn't a strong enough argument for me not to have [a child] in my life.''

It was the right decision for her, but it was still a brave one to make. Her image, as she knew, was almost squeaky-clean, a role model for young women, and this would alter that. Sometimes the personal had to come before the political—but at the same time, this was a political decision. The traditional nuclear family with its ''family values'' certainly hadn't always worked. And around her she had a strong network of support, in Rohan and her parents, who would be behind her every step of the way. The life she was carrying inside her and that she would bring to term, would have a strong musical and political heritage, both from her and from the Marley side. But, most importantly, the baby would have love.

Meanwhile, the Fugees had commitments in 1997, things that Lauryn wanted to honor. Obviously, she couldn't keep touring indefinitely—it would simply be too great a strain on her—but for the moment, as long as she was careful, things would be fine. At least they were off the road for a while, so she was finally able to get some rest, and keep her strength up, which was important.

During the break, Clef was hard at work, down in the Basement finishing off a solo album. While some of the tunes had become staples of the Fugees' set, like a cover of the old song, ''Guantanamera,'' this was a very personal project with very strong ties to his Haitian background. As a band, the Fugees were exhausted from being on the road for so long, and not at their creative best as a trio. But Wyclef had songs inside that he wanted to release that didn't necessarily come within the scope of the group.

Lauryn, who would appear on the album with Pras, was supportive of the venture. ''A lot of what's on this album is a chapter out of Wyclef's life,'' she said, ''or out of our collective lives. I know this because I know Clef personally, and I know exactly what he went through to get to this place in his life. And there's still growth going on.''

Much of the recording had been done on the road, in studios as far apart as Paris and Trinidad. He sent the finished tracks down to Haiti, where they could be played on the radio, which left a lot of people wary of bootlegging—the album wouldn't be out for several months yet. But, as Clef pointed out, people there wanted to hear the music, and for most of them a radio was all they could afford; they didn't have the money for CDs and CD players. They were lucky if they had enough for food.

January gave the group collectively a huge boost, when the Grammy nominations appeared, and they had two, for Best Rap Album (for *The Score)*, and Best R&B Performance by a Duo or Group (for ''Killing Me Softly With His Song''). They'd also been asked to perform at the Grammy show, which could only increase their audience.

Things continued to happen in Lauryn's own life, too. The baby was growing inside her, causing some cravings (a weakness for gritty foods). And she'd been asked to undertake another movie role. Her past experience hadn't exactly been in serious cinema, but this would be—an adaptation of Toni Morrison's novel, *Beloved.* Tempting as it was to get a serious acting credential, between her schedule with the band and her pregnancy she was forced to refuse. It was a shame, because the movie would have been a perfect fit for her. But it wasn't as if there was a shortage of scripts coming into the brick house in South Orange. With her photogenic looks, she was something of a natural . . . and it was apparent from the videos that the camera loved her. That she could act, and had done so professionally, was almost the icing on the cake for a director or a studio—although it was a prerequisite for her. She was a professional, and to be anything less would have been a complete insult.

She was in front of the camera again in February, when the Grammy show was broadcast live, first performing with the crew, then join-ing Pras and Clef at the podium as they ac-cepted the awards for Best Rap Album and Best R&B Performance by a Duo or Group.

The trophies were the industry's way of ac-knowledging what they'd done. The massive sales of *The Score* had given the industry a real shot, and more importantly for the long-term, they'd helped bring hip-hop into the main-stream. To the business, that was probably their greatest achievement, and its effects would be massive. With the dam broken, hip-hop album after hip-hop album would go to the top of the charts.

From there, it was back to Europe again. This time, even more than on the last trip, they came as conquering heroes. In England, that meant two nights playing to sold-out crowds at Wembley Arena—well over 40,000 people, all told. Those crowds were echoed wherever they played in Europe. They'd graduated to the very big time, the level few bands achieve. The tour was timed to hit London to coincide with the Brit Awards, where the Fugees had been nom-inated for, and ended up winning, one of the trophies.

However, this tour would only be a prelude to something that would achieve a dream of Wyclef's—the Fugees were going to play in Haiti, his homeland. It was important to realize just how big a national figure Wyclef Jean had become in the country of his birth. It was a land that had become perceived internationally as the home of voodoo, dictators, and AIDS. The people were dirt-poor, ground down by regimes that had barely treated them as human.

A few changes had taken place, but for the most part, Haiti had a fairly negative international image. It was a place of history, and the people had a very fierce dignity. But it was a country devoid of heroes. Geographically, Haiti occupied part of an island, sharing it with another country, the Dominican Republic. That hardly ranked as one of the world's richest countries, but thanks to some successful ballplayers and a more democratic outlook on politics, it seemed a much more positive and thriving place.

So for Haiti to produce someone who was internationally renowned and respected was a very big deal. Wyclef was the native son who had made good, and who hadn't forgotten his roots. He'd become something of a national celebrity (it hadn't happened to the same extent with Pras, in part because he'd been born in America, and carried a U.S. passport). When he spoke, people in Port-au-Prince and all the towns around wanted to hear his words. To them, anything from Clef was important. It was one of the reasons he'd been willing to send down tracks from his solo record, without any real care as to whether it was bootlegged. For Haiti's youth—which make up some forty percent of the population—he was a role model. He knew his record was going to sell in America when it was released. In Haiti, he could afford to give something away.

"If your records ain't selling, it's because you lack creativity," he said. "It's not because a hundred thousand kids bootlegged your CD. My interest has always been to appeal to those with nothing. That can't change just because the Fugees is big." That meant responsibility, and he wanted to give something back to the country that had given him life. A concert was one of his solutions. Organizing it was far from straightforward, even with the support of Prime Minister Rene Preval. There were still plenty of logistical hurdles to be overcome: organizing bands, both Haitian and international, equipment, and what would be the most important thing for Clef, what to do with the profits from the concert, which had been set for April 1997. Following Lauryn's example, he'd set up the Wyclef Jean Foundation, whose mission was to help Haitian youth around the word, the refugees at home and abroad. "My dream is to get Wyclef Jean buildings, just like they have YMCA buildings, in Brooklyn and in Little Haiti in Miami."

The concert was going to be a massive affair, the culmination of several days that the band would spend in the country (which would all be documented by a film crew from Minneapolis, for possible future distribution, as well as by local television, and by MTV). Its aim was to bring unity to the Haitian people, and to focus the attention of the media, specifically the American media, on them in a positive light for once. "The Jews have their stories, the Sicilians have their stories, and we have our stories," Clef explained. "In actuality, it's all really the same story. Everyone was the slave of someone—whether you're white, black, Chinese. We're all the same family." And that family was set to convene in Port-au-Prince on April 12.

When the band landed at the airport on April 9, they were greeted, not only by thousands of fans, but also by the Prime Minister, Rosny Smarth, and Paoul Peck, the Minister of Culture. In a welcoming speech, Smarth declaimed, "The Fugees have been a shot in the arm . . . it shows us there's still a lot worthwhile in this country, and that we have just as many serious and committed people as we have hooligans and con men." The President presented Clef with the National Order of Honor, and in acceptance Clef said, "We're representing the street kids here who can't get into the Presidential Palace. We came down here for the kids. Their welcome was unbelievable. But we need to show them that they have to respect and educate themselves.''

Clef's ''Yon Chans'' seemed to be always playing everywhere on Haitian radio. While Clef was the Haitian figurehead, Pras, with his background, was something of a celebrity, as was Lauryn. They spent their days touring children's charities, seeing the work that was being done, and assessing what would be needed in the future.

On the tenth they traveled to northern Haiti, where they played a show at the Magic Haiti Club Med, an exclusive resort, with tickets costing $100 each. What the gig brought in would all go to the charities, but Clef was incensed by the very fact that it was happening, and what they were really doing was entertaining vacationers. ''How come there's no one here from Cite Soleil?'' he asked, referring to Haiti's largest ghetto in Port-au-Prince. ''How would they get in if they came?''

He'd always insisted that the band's music was for everyone, but if it focused on any particular segment of society, it was the underclass, not those who were sleek and well-fed.

But he'd have chance to rectify the situation a couple of days later. The show, called ''Coming Home,'' was sponsored by the Ministry of

Culture, and set for the Bicentenaire, Port-au-Prince's biggest stadium. It would feature not only the Fugees, but a number of other acts, including Haiti's own Boukman Eksperyans, one of the few groups that had made any kind of international impression. At one time their very political lyrics had brought them trouble. Now they were folk heroes to an extent, standing up and telling the truth.

Throughout the morning people streamed into the arena. In Haiti, with its volatile society, a big crowd could mean trouble. But these people were here to enjoy themselves, not to cause trouble. The estimates of the numbers there ranged between 50,000 and 100,000, with most people agreeing that 80,000 was a fairly accurate figure. It was far more than the government had expected. "It felt great," Clef said later. "It shook the country up, because I don't think anyone expected 80,000 people to show up for one concert. When other rappers talk about being Gambinos and other types of Mafia-type people, I laugh. You wouldn't know my power until I go to Haiti and there are 3,000 soldiers behind me, my age, carrying Uzis, waiting for me to make my move. It felt beautiful for my father to leave for political reasons, and for me, a rebel son, to return and be treated like a hero."

However much they enjoyed the other acts,

the focus of the audience was on the Fugees, and after some four hours of listening to the rest, the headliners took the stage for what was really their biggest-ever show, not just in terms of numbers, but, more importantly, significance. And they were quite determined to make this into an event to be remembered. One thing this would *not* be was a quick run through the hits and then off the stage, into the limo, and back to the hotel. They were here to entertain the have-nots, to create memories for them that would last a lifetime. And they were in no hurry to leave the stage, playing for almost four hours in the sweltering April heat. Of course all the hits were there, but they were just the tip of the iceberg. On two of the cuts from his upcoming solo album, ''Yele'' and ''San Feze'' (''Without Guns'') already familiar to those listening, Clef sang in his first tongue, Creole, to the obvious delight of everyone. Then there was ''Gunpowder,'' one of Clef's early compositions, which Lauryn had first sung with him seven years before, and which they'd recorded with the I-Threes on backing vocals after meeting them at a Grammy rehearsal.

''It was incredible,'' Lauryn said of the recording session. ''They heard and sang the song for the first time when they got to the studio. And it was just like having the spirit of

Bob Marley there, like a blessing." But she had Marley's spirit inside her, too, growing bigger every day.

"Yon Chans" got everybody moving, and then the Cuban anthem, "Guantanamera" (which Clef had recorded for his album with Pras and Cuban singing legend Celia Cruz), kept them on their feet. "For me, 'Guantanamera' just keeps tying in the links between blacks and Latinos and everyone else to make hearing it feel like they are one," Clef explained. Then it was all the way to the climax, with the best known tunes from *The Score*, "Ready or Not," "Zealots," "How Many Mics," and the ultimate finale, a full-on version of "No Woman, No Cry," which just couldn't have been topped. As evening turned into night, the Fugees left the stage, having given their all to a crowd that fully appreciated it.

And then it was all over. One of the biggest events in the history of Haiti was finished. At least, the entertainment side of it was done. The business side had just begun. Clef knew that that would be an even greater battle than actually setting up the concert, and at a press conference before leaving the country, he issued his warning to the people: "Tomorrow, I'll be on a plane back to New York. Watch where the money goes."

His suspicions seemed to be justified. When the Haitian government finally released the figures, they claimed that the concert's gross of $300,000 had just covered the costs of staging it. It was something that many Haitians, including Clef, greatly doubted, and he said so. "The government could do something like that, and no one could prove anything." Even a hero might find it hard to topple an entrenched regime. Still, it didn't stop him staging a similar concert a year later, once again to benefit Haitian refugees. But this time he made sure it was staged in Miami.

Wyclef's album, *Presents The Carnival featuring Refugee Allstars*, appeared in June 1997, with Lauryn and Pras named as co-executive producers with Clef himself. But Lauryn's involvement didn't end there. She was featured on several tracks, and as well as her voice, she lent writing credits to "Year of the Dragon" (and also additional lyrics for "Guantanamera," a true ghetto tale). "Sang Fezi," sung in Creole, was something very different, very minimal and Haitian in its feel, and one of the songs the crowd had absolutely loved in Port-au-Prince. It connected the line between Haiti and Brooklyn. It featured Lauryn's singing, rather than her rhyming skills, and was an excellent demonstration of how soulful she could sound, over chord changes that were taken from the old blues song "House of the Rising Sun." "Gunpowder," of course, had been recorded that year, with that I-Three backing vocal. A beautiful acoustic piece, it was really in the tradition of Bob Marley, and when Lauryn's voice shadowed Clef's, it was the kind of thing that could send shivers up the spine.

For a woman getting closer to her due date every day, Lauryn hadn't eased up on her commitments. The Fugees had also contributed a track to the soundtrack of *When We Were Kings*, the movie produced by their manager, David Sonenberg, about the Muhammed Ali—George Foreman "Rumble in the Jungle" heavyweight title fight that was staged in Zaire in 1974, along with a concert that was billed as an African Woodstock, and certainly featured some heavy hitters of its own, including the Godfather of Soul himself, James Brown; B.B. King; and the Spinners. Along with A Tribe Called Quest, Busta Rhymes, and Forte, the Fugees wrote and performed "Rumble in the Jungle," which was produced by Clef and Lauryn, who had developed her own reputation for knowing how to get some great sounds in the studio. The song contained, incongruously, a sample from Abba's "The Name of the Game" (actually the bassline), and an interpolation of "Angel of the Morning," the sixties country hit. It was some high-quality hip-hop, and L gave it on the mic, a little history lesson, as well as some singing, particularly her rewritten version of "Angel of the Morning."

Released as a single in Britain, "Rumble in the Jungle" proved that the Fugees had become an unstoppable force, going all the way to number 3. The film had premiered at Radio City Music Hall in February, with Ali himself, now older and sick, as the guest of honor. There, the Fugees had joined blues legend B.B. King onstage for two numbers, both sung directly to Muhammed Ali (who'd been something of a role model for black youth, having changed his name from Cassius Clay after winning the world heavyweight title in the sixties, then refusing to go and serve in Vietnam).

"Rumble in the Jungle" couldn't exactly be called a new Fugees track, since they made up only part of the crew on it. But another soundtrack, to the movie *love jones*, really did contain some new Fugees material. *love jones* was Theodore Witcher's directorial debut, set around a Chicago nightclub, the Sanctuary, where poet and writer Darius (Larenz Tate) met photographer Nina (Nia Long). He was besotted with her, but she was a bit more wary, having just been dumped. Eventually she succumbed, although they both insisted it was just a "sex thing." But love raised its head, and their affair was the meat of the picture.

The *Refugee Camp All-Stars*—essentially the Fugees—offered "The Sweetest Thing," written by and featuring Lauryn, and produced by her and Wyclef. It was most definitely a change of direction, a lovely slow jam that seemed to hark back to the jazzier style of someone like Nina Simone, albeit with some definite hip-hop flourishes, like the scratching that moved the song from section to section. It was Lauryn getting even more of a chance to show what she could do vocally than she'd had on *The Score*, and she handled it beautifully, mellifluously, and with a great deal of subtlety. Released as a single—it was the most obviously commercial new track on the record, and the Fugees name meant automatic sales—it charted. Would this be one future direction for the band? They'd always brought in many elements, but never shown that jazzy side so heavily. Or was it all Lauryn's influence? Time would tell.

But just after the middle of the year, there were other things on Lauryn's mind. The Fugees were off the road, unable to tour because of her pregnancy, and the baby was due.

It was something of a true multi-cultural birth. Rohan was there, of course, as was Valerie Hill, Lauryn's assistant, Dieynaba, a Jamaican midwife, and her obstetrician. "My doctor had this really strong accent. He's from Israel. And Dieynaba has a very West African-French accent. So my mother was like, 'Girl, push! C'mon, girl, push!' And Dieynaba was like 'Push, dah'ling. Oh push, dah'ling, push.' And my Jamaican midwife was like, 'Push, gal! Yuh ha fi push it out! Push, push!' And my doctor was totally nonchalant like, 'Oh, push, push, push.' It was hilarious.'' Looking back, it was easy for her to see it as hilarious, but at the time it was a very serious business indeed, and as painful as only childbirth can be. But she delivered a healthy young boy, Zion, into the world, and counted her blessings that everything had gone perfectly.

With the birth, Lauryn's whole world changed. For the last few years, the Fugees had been the focus of her life, the band occupying almost all her waking moments. Now she had another human being to look after and nurture, and he became the central point of her life. A new life, a new beginning.

seven

But even before Zion was born, there had been new beginnings for Lauryn. The pregnancy had spurred her creativity, and she began writing songs at a furious pace, working in the attic where she could still look out and see the sunlight on the buildings of the project, not as golden and magical as it had seemed when she was a child, but still powerful nonetheless. Altogether, she penned thirty songs very quickly, including one for gospel great CeCe Winans, which was recorded right as Lauryn was due to give birth, with Lauryn finding the concentration to also produce the track.

"I had so much energy, I was bouncing off the walls," she recalled. "We were in the studio, singing and dancing to a song I wrote called 'On That Day,' and the very next day my little man showed up. He totally refocused me, gave me something to love as much as anything else I could love.''

Every priority changed, and with parenthood came plenty of new insights.

''When I was a teenager, I used to be really critical when I'd think about how the civil rights movement went so far and basically stopped, and I'd think, 'Where did your fire go?' Now I know what happened. Everyone had kids. And that's the challenge: maintaining that fire, knowing that the sacrifice is different now; it's not just you. But I'm a fighter, and I want my son to be a fighter. I want him to be comfortable, but I don't want to lose my fire and passion.''

There seemed to be little danger of her losing either of those things. Within just a few months of Zion's birth, she was in Detroit, accompanied by Valerie Hill, to work with soul legend Aretha Franklin, a woman who had influenced her vocally. Lauryn had offered Aretha one of her songs, ''A Rose is Still a Rose,'' and the legend had decided to record it, making it the single and the album's title track. Not only that, she made her directorial debut with the accompanying video. ''Aretha's so baaad,'' Lauryn said. ''When I wrote the song—the rhythm, the syncopation is definitely hip-hop— I expected to have to really go through it with her. But she took the demo version, came in the studio, and it was done.'' Aretha herself was impressed with Lauryn. ''She's positive, detailed, conscientious. Frankly, I was surprised to see that in such a young woman.''

Two things seemed quite notable in Lauryn's life, however, as 1997 progressed. The first was that, even after Zion's birth, she refrained from naming his father, even though Rohan remained very much a presence in her life, for which was eternally grateful. But the father's identity was part of her private life, not to be pored over by the public. ''I felt like the world had enough of me,'' she said. ''I felt like I put my soul on records, and I didn't have to answer any global questions about who my boyfriend was.''

The other thing was that Lauryn was obviously doing more work on her own, away from the other members of the Fugees. To be fair, Clef had released *The Carnival*, which had gone multi-platinum and would end up being nominated for two Grammy awards, and that had been somewhat apart from the group. But now Lauryn's artistic work seemed well removed from the Refugee camp, which was leading to speculation that the Fugees might no longer even exist, although nothing was being officially said.

Most certainly there seemed to be a growing

distance emotionally between the three of them, even though they all had homes in the same part of New Jersey (Clef also had a penthouse apartment in Manhattan, although his wife lived in the New Jersey house). A lot of that had been brought about by the incessant touring and the interviews that went with it. While Clef and Pras would be quizzed on their political views, the questions offered to Lauryn would be much softer, and her bandmates did nothing to change that. "I guess I just got fed up with being seen as the token female in the Fugees," she said. Men have a way of taking away the self-respect women have, often with just the smallest of comments. And, she added, "It was as if my opinion didn't matter at all. And it was strange because the three of us as a group aren't like that, but I just felt relegated by the men talking shop all the time."

At the same time, she didn't lay the blame completely at the doors of Pras and Clef. She realized that much of the responsibility lay with others, including those who'd advised her to go solo after *Blunted on Reality*. ". . . It did cause some strain. I think it made [Wyclef and Pras] feel like they had to champion other agendas. Like, just in case I did jump ship, everybody else was going to be all right." And, she also admitted, there was an element of competitiveness within the band, which had to be inevitable when three such creative people came together.

Whatever the root cause, it seemed as if it wasn't going to be resolved anytime soon. At the same time, no one seemed to be ruling out a future Fugees album (and at the time of writing, there had been rumors of one appearing in 1999, although with the success of *The Miseducation of Lauryn Hill*, that would seem to be a very hopeful time frame).

However, 1998 opened in a way no one expected, with a new track from the Fugees, on a record no one would ever have anticipated them being on—*Elmopalooza!* Broadcast on February 20, it was a *Sesame Street* special, helping to mark the show's thirtieth anniversary. A take-off of the Lollapalooza festivals, the characters from the show sang with different artists and the Fugees got to collaborate with Big Bird. The show, and its accompanying album, was a strange mix of talents. Also offering tracks were Gloria Estefan, En Vogue, The Mighty Mighty Bosstones, Rosie O'Donnell, Shawn Colvin, Aerosmith's Steven Tyler, Jimmy Buffett, Celine Dion, and Kenny Loggins.

But who could refuse an offer to be on *Sesame Street*? Both Lauryn and Pras had grown up with the program that had helped educate and entertain a few generations of America's pre-schoolers. And it had always promoted positive values, the kind of things the Fugees stood for—as did the other artists in their own ways. A song from the show, "Happy to be Me," had been written in 1993 by Gail Sky King, and was performed by the Fugees in their inimitable fashion. Certainly no one had managed to reproduce their sound yet. And for Lauryn, now a parent herself, there was a special resonance about being able to do something that would help entertain her own son.

Musically, the track made no concessions to a younger audience. This was vintage Fugees, melodic hip-hop, with Lauryn singing (and speaking the chorus), while the band made the verses into a rap. Perhaps it shouldn't have worked (and it was hilarious to hear Clef singing about being in his pajamas and drinking orange juice), but it did, with a strong hip-hop beat and sounding as inviting as *The Score*'s loveliest tracks, like "Fu-Gee-La" or "Ready or Not." "I produced the track," Clef said. "It went great." The recorded version was just the Fugees, though, without Big Bird, who'd been unable to make the session in New Jersey. It was a sidetrack, an odd track, and certainly no indication that the Fugees were still a working band. Clef was on the road with the Refugee All Stars (including Pras, but definitely no Lauryn) when the special aired. But it did give the band a much more human, and less serious face, to show and an indication of the warmth they felt toward the next generation, as well as illustrating that hip-hop was a music with many facets, and didn't all have to be strident, loud, and gangsta-oriented.

Becoming a mother seemed to sharpen Lauryn's skills, and also her desires to do even more than just parent. It was as if she felt she had to do it all, to prove that a woman could be more than one thing at a time. Certainly she had the ambition. Long before, she'd stated that she assumed that she'd do a solo record at some point. The question was, had she reached the point where she felt that desire strongly enough? That was something she had to mull over. She had the songs, even if, like "A Rose is Still a Rose" and "On That Day," they'd originally been intended for other singers, and she had the experience in the studio to make them into something very real. There was absolutely no doubt that the label would welcome a solo album from her with open arms. Those were the outside factors. The internal factor was much more important. Did she want to do it? And, with Zion around, could she split her energies between him and the creative process while doing justice to them both?

She understood that she'd been very naive in the past, but that was then, when she'd been younger. Success had versed her much more, both in the way of the business and the way of the world. If she was going to undertake a venture like a record, it would be serious, not some throwaway. She had things to say. "I take my music seriously. There's nothing fictional about what I'm doing. Everything I write, everything I say, is a profession. . . . my role is to communicate what I experience to the greater world."

One thing she wouldn't do was let anyone else make up her mind for her, or put any pressure on her. Whatever she did would be done in her own time, with her own motivation, not at the behest of some record company. People were telling her that she really should make a solo album, but no one could agree on what kind of album she should make. Some suggested that she should sing, others that she should stick with hip-hop. About the only thing Lauryn knew for certain was that, if she did decide to record, it would be her own approach, picking up a lot on what she'd learned with the Fugees, neither all one thing nor all the other.

Finally, she knew she was ready to decide, and she knew that she had to let all the music that was welling up inside her come out. She could juggle her commitments, and with Rohan and her mother around, Zion wouldn't exactly be neglected. Ruffhouse, and particularly its parent company, Columbia, was happy to have her back in the studio. But before any recording began, there were still a few details to be sorted out.

Lauryn was adamant that this would be *her* album. That meant she'd be doing the writing, the arranging, *and* the producing. It wouldn't be filled with superstar guests to try and sell a few more copies. It would stand or fall on the quality of the music within. In terms of production, there had been some talk of bringing in an outside producer—RZA of Wu-Tang Clan had been mentioned as a possible person behind the board—but she refused. "It would have been more difficult to articulate to other people," Lauryn noted, and then said elsewhere, "Hey, it's my album. Who can tell my story better than me?", both of which were perfectly justifiable points. Certainly Columbia dismissed any rumors that they'd tried to impose an outside producer on her. Her experience, with the Fugees and with CeCe Winans, spoke for itself. The woman knew exactly what she was doing.

It was a big step, and a big responsibility, but still quite small when compared to the biggest responsibility in her life, her son. That was major. An album was important, but against a life, it meant nothing. A life was by far the more important thing, and Lauryn wanted Zion to be a part of the experience of her music-making wherever possible, taking him with her when that was feasible.

The Fugees had done a lot to change the entire face of hip-hop. But a lot of people had assumed that much of the distinctive sound had been because of Clef's particular vision, his blending of musics. He, however, had only been one-third of the band. Chris Schwartz, the CEO of Ruffhouse, knew better. "I don't think a lot of people gave Lauryn credit for how much she contributed to *The Score*," he said. "A lot of people assumed that she was just the singer. I think when this new album comes out, she's really going to get her due as an artist."

That was a big claim, but he'd been there, he'd been involved from the very beginning, and was as familiar as anyone outside the band could have been. He knew what to expect of Lauryn, and what she expected of herself. She'd been part of a group that had set the standard, and now she was planning on more than living up to it. That was her way.

"The first day in the studio, I think I ordered every instrument I ever fell in love with: harps, strings, timpani drums, organ, clarinets . . . It was my idea to record it so the human element stayed in. I didn't want it to be too technically perfect.'' In a digital age, a perfection of sound, that sonic sheen, was quite easily achieved. Even a single wrong note could be overdubbed. And in hip-hop, most of the backing tracks tended to come from carefully amended samples, manipulated by computer technology. Technology, in fact, although it had improved the quality of the audio, and the abilities of the musicians to truly record what they heard in their heads, had taken some of the life out of music. Analogue sounds were much warmer than digital sounds, many people agreed, and however good, say, a synthesized version of a Hammond organ sounded, there was something missing.

On *The Score* the Fugees had mixed it all up, using samples from records along with live instruments, taking elements from older songs and reworking them within their own vision. Clef had done it on *The Carnival*, too, and it was the way Lauryn wanted her own music to be—a new hybrid, but always fueled by the sound of real musicians playing the instruments they loved in the studio.

It wasn't going to be easy for her, she knew that. Did the people who bought hip-hop albums, and those who'd be buying this, even care whether there were ''real'' instruments on a track anymore? ''The anxiety of this project was the fear that we would have been so used to fast food [music], that if you give them something that came from the soul and the heart, they would want McDonald's, basically," she explained.

For Lauryn, there was never any doubt that this record would contain a lot of soul. It was the music she'd grown up on, on those days in the attic when she played her way through her mother's record collection. Along with the gospel she heard in church, it had been her formative musical influence, before the sounds of hip-hop had changed her perspective. Now she had a chance to make her own soul record. Nothing retro, still very nineties, but with a real feel, and a real truth about it. The last thing she wanted to consider as she settled down in the studio was whether it would be a hit or not.

"There's too much pressure to have hits today," she said. "Artists are watching *Billboard* instead of exploring their environment . . . Look at someone like Aretha. She didn't hit with her first album, but she was able to grow up and find herself. I want to make honest music. I don't like things to be too perfect, too polished. People may criticize me for that, but I grew up listening to singers like Al Green and Sam Cooke. When they hit a high note, you really felt it."

The idea of creativity had largely been replaced by an emphasis on the bottom line, which she was determined to ignore. The Fugees had gone with their hearts, and the success and money followed. If they went with her again, fine, but she was still going to make the record that satisfied her.

"Our podium, what we have to speak from, is the music. It's really important that we stay focused, because things become misconstrued in the media. So we have to stick firm to who we are, and stand our ground musically. We have to make sure the music and the message and the words and all the elements come through in our songs and every time we appear in public . . . A lot of us are too busy focusing on what we think people want to hear, as opposed to just saying what's in our hearts."

The album would be something of a narrative, in many ways about a relationship, because "I think every woman goes through a relationship which is a great lesson in love." Lauryn herself had gone through one before meeting Rohan, and the songs she'd written afterward helped work it through her system, and brought her to a new place, mentally and emotionally.

The title of it was already in her mind, *The Miseducation of Lauryn Hill*, a reference to the relationship where she learned a lot, much of it bad. But it was also an homage to the 1974 film directed by Michael Campus, *The Edu-*

cation of Sonny Carson, from Carson's auto-biographical book, a harrowing no-holds-barred look at his adolescence in Brooklyn, growing up amid drugs, prostitution, and crime. And there was another, more direct reference to Carter G. Woodson's book, *The Miseducation of the Negro.* She'd learned too much, in school and out of it, and was too political, not to throw those things at people. If they understood, fine. If they didn't, that was fine, too. Perhaps they might look a little deeper and so discover something.

She also understood that although this was her record, some of the people working with her on it might not take her directing them too easily, and she was prepared for that.

"Men have a hard time taking direction from women, but when you pay somebody, you pay them to get it right . . . So I don't pay attention to that at all. Music is so important to me and how I come across in music is so important. I'm a perfectionist. If I have to do it a hundred times, I'll do it a hundred times!"

The initial sessions would be laid down at Chung King Studios in New York, which Clef had used for his album. The three of them might no longer be playing together, but it was impossible to shake all the ties; they'd seen too much water go under the bridge together for that. But it was important that neither Clef nor

Pras, nor any of the Fugees crew for that matter, be involved in this, so it could be seen as Lauryn's venture, so it would be judged by what *she* did. Although she didn't want it full of big names, two major performers would lend a hand. "I Used to Love Him" would feature Mary J. Blige, and "Nothing Even Matters" would have the vocal talents of D'Angelo helping out.

The biggest surprise, though, was the inclusion of Carlos Santana on the track Lauryn had written about her baby, "To Zion." Guitarist Santana had led the band that bore his name for some three decades, among the very first to put a Latin groove into rock music. To find him working with someone so involved in hip-hop seemed a strange juxtaposition to many, but not to Lauryn herself.

"I've always adored Carlos Santana and considered him a true master," she explained. "It actually started out for me when I was little. I had his *Abraxas* album. This is how I'm as weird as I am. I was fooling around. . . . one day, I think I was six or seven years old, and I found a forty-five [record]." And the song with its lovely changes—as she pointed out, so many songs these days didn't have changes, or bridges—fit his very fluid style. Just because it was hip-hop didn't exclude Santana from being able to play to it, any more than the rhythm had stopped Aretha singing "A Rose is Still a Rose."

"There's no reason why Carlos Santana can't pick to the hip-hop drums, because he's a musician."

She had a very definite idea about musicality, about the arts of songwriting and arranging. Where there were drums, she wanted them to be hard, and she wanted the songs to sound like songs, with changes and melody, like the old soul and R&B songs had. As star, producer, and arranger, she was responsible for every part, and that was exactly what she needed. It wasn't just a case of going into the studio, laying down a vocal, then going home. Her apprenticeship with the Fugees—for it seemed as if all that she'd learned with them had been leading up to this—had served her very well. Theirs had been a hands-on partnership, learning as they went, not from theory, but by doing, by being unafraid to break the rules. What Lauryn wanted from people might sometimes have gone against conventional wisdom, but she was in charge. Unlike the Fugees, this wasn't a democracy. When she was in the studio, it was Lauryn's fiefdom. In fact, there would be only two tracks where she wasn't solely responsible for the production: "To Zion," which was co-produced by Che Guevara, and "Lost Ones," which had a co-production credit for Vada Nobles. The album's title track would have a credit for additional musical contribution by Tejumold Newton, while Johari Newton would be credited with additional lyrical contributions on "Everything is Everything" and "Superstar," with James Poyser making a musical contribution to "Superstar."

There was absolutely nothing wrong with that. Sometimes a more objective eye, or in this case ear, could see things that Lauryn herself could, immersed as she was in the project. That was sometimes the reason for using an outside producer, simply because that person could look at everything more dispassionately. However, when a person had such a clear vision of what they wanted, as Lauryn did in this instance, an outside producer for the whole album would have been pointless.

The studio work in New York had begun toward the end of 1997. Used as she'd been to working in the relaxed pace of Booga Basement, playing with friends, people she knew very, very well, the sessions this time were a bit more stressful. This wasn't her studio, where she could stretch out and experiment. Instead there were schedules to keep, players to be paid. Lauryn wasn't the only one using the studio, or the only musician on the album (instrumentally, her credits were limited to vocals), so she couldn't come and go as she pleased. She was working in parameters put up by others, which was a little different for her, but after a short while she adapted to the new situation. If anything, it made her even more focused and concentrated. With less time, and a little less freedom, she had to hit it quicker, to demand more from everyone else and herself—and she wasn't afraid to do that.

New York would be the place where the bulk of the work on the album would be done. But Chung King wasn't the only studio where she'd end up working. There was also Sony Studios, the complex the label had put together where its artists could record, and which also included a soundstage and video facilities, everything in one place, RPM, and Right Track. Sometimes one track would have different elements added at different studios. And then there was also Perfect Pair Studios, much closer to home in New Jersey, away from the hubbub and distraction of Manhattan. There was even one track (''Final Hour'') that was partially recorded at George Martin's Air Studios in London, a place that always gave a good sound.

There was one other place where Lauryn wanted to do some recording, though, where she felt the vibe would be absolutely perfect for the type of album she was making. It wasn't in New York or New Jersey. It wasn't even in America. It was Marley Music, Inc., located in Kingston, Jamaica, the studio built by Bob Marley, Rohan's father, and Zion's grandfather.

She went down and started work there in the fall of '97, situating herself at 56 Hope Road. She, Rohan, and Zion would be back on the island later, at the Reggae Sunsplash festival, held every year in the resort of Ocho Rios. It would also be a celebration of what would have been Marley's fifty-third birthday, had he lived, and the members of his family were gathering to celebrate the event—so Lauryn, who was definitely a Marley, even if not in name or marriage, had to be there.

Sunsplash was always a major event, bringing in the best talent in Jamaican music, and visitors from around the world who appreciated the music. It was Lauryn's first time, but with so much of this particular event focusing on Robert Nesta Marley, she felt quite at home. Perhaps the highlight of the whole festival was the set by Ziggy Marley and the Melody Makers, the band formed by some of Bob's children, which had first hit big in the late eighties, with Ziggy sounding uncannily like his late father, and the band continuing the line of "conscious", rootsy reggae.

On this night, they had some very special

guests on the stage with them: the I-Threes, who'd worked with the Fugees before. Rita Marley (Bob's widow), Marcia Griffith, and Judy Mowatt had all gone on to attain reputations as vocalists in their own right, but as Bob's backing singers, they'd helped spark the magic in his music. Now they were singing the songs again with a new generation.

Before the set, the entire Marley family had crossed to the festival site in wooden boats painted in the Rasta colors of red, gold, and green, the symbolic colors of Africa. Lauryn had been part of the family. Backstage, she hung out with the band and the family, Rohan and Zion close by, and then she joined the Melody Makers as they played, being introduced and hailed in her own right, as a fellow spirit come to pay homage.

"Happy birthday, Bob Marley," she said, before remembering "my newborn son" and amending her words to "Happy birthday, Grandpa! Respect!"

It was a joyous moment for everyone, but it was also the first time that Lauryn had confirmed concretely that Rohan was, indeed, Zion's father, even though the rumor mongers seemed to have made up their minds after the boy's birth.

Sunsplash was the fun part of the trip, and the chance for the Marley clan to congregate was reason enough to fly down to Jamaica, to honor the legend and life of Bob Marley. His spirit might well have been there in Ocho Rios, but Lauryn was hoping it had also been in Kingston the previous fall when she was recording there.

Marley's studio had seen the creation of so much classic music, songs that had inspired, and still could, the songs of love and revolution. He'd been an influence on the Fugees, and most especially on Lauryn, whose ties to him were now closer than ever. Maybe she'd never achieve the same heights that he had, where the music she was making lived on and traveled around the world, from Africa to America and Europe, crossing over generational boundaries, but that was her ultimate aim. Marley had mixed art and politics, and that was what Lauryn, too, had been doing throughout her career. So just to be recording in the studio where much of that work had been put on tape was more than a thrill; it was awe-inspiring.

It meant, too, that she'd be working with some of Jamaica's top musicians, like guitarist Earl ''Chinna'' Smith, who'd contributed his guitar work to the remake of ''No Woman No Cry,'' and Dean Frasier, who had a reputation for his sax work both in reggae and jazz. Another reggae legend, Al Anderson, who'd played in the Wailers with Bob Marley, would also be on the record, but recorded in New York, not Kingston (he would appear on the track "Nothing Even Matters"), but it all helped cinch tighter the connections Lauryn felt to Marley. Even when it was immediately evident, Lauryn knew that the revolutionary spirit of real roots reggae ran through her music, a parallel to the love she had for old soul music, which could also be quite revolutionary, as in Marvin Gaye's *What's Going On?* or the work of Gil Scott-Heron. All she was doing was continuing a tradition and putting her own stamp on it.

The Tuff Gong studio, as it was known, had a warm, welcoming feel, exactly what Lauryn needed after the rush of New York. It relaxed and opened her, musically and personally.

"It was our first morning in Jamaica, and I saw all these kids gathered around Lauryn, screaming and dancing," remembered Gordon Williams, known on the disc as Commissioner Gordon, the recording engineer throughout. "Lauryn was in the living room next to the studio with about fifteen Marley grandchildren around her—the children of Ziggy and Stephen and Julian—and she starts singing this rap verse, and all the kids are repeating the last word of each line, chiming in very spontaneously because they were so into the song."

The song was "Lost Ones," which would be the first cut on the record, and the words had come to her a few minutes before, inspired by a drum machine pattern that had given her a rhythm, and then some words to match. She knew immediately that the three weeks she'd be spending in Kingston would be fruitful. And to complete the reggae connection, she had the thought of including a sample of "Bam Bam" by Toots and the Maytals (written by Freddie "Toots" Hibbert), contemporaries of Bob Marley from the ska era onward, in the song.

Truth to tell, the sessions at Tuff Gong gave Lauryn the fire and desire to really push ahead. She'd had her ideas and her tracks before she went to Jamaica, but the atmosphere there jolted her creativity, and gave a real form to both the subject of the album, and the way it was constructed. Even Williams, who worked closely with her on every session, wasn't sure how it would all come together; it was like a puzzle in Lauryn's head, gradually taking shape.

Something that had to be an element in it all for her was gospel music. As she pointed out, when gospel music is mentioned, the majority of people immediately think of choirs, praise singing, hands clapping, and people being moved by the Spirit. "But gospel music is music inspired by the Gospels," she said. "In a huge respect, a lot of this music turned out to be that. During this album, I turned to the Bible and wrote songs that I drew comfort from, because I lost my grandmother, my cousin, a seven-year-old friend—a lot of people close to me.''

The concept of the album, though firm in her mind, kept changing in detail as she wrote, refined, and recorded, and she knew it. ''The meaning of the title, *The Miseducation of Lauryn Hill*, has grown since I wrote the album. It ended up saying a lot about what people didn't know about me. A lot of people around me did not know who I really was.'' It was personal, and written to exorcise a lot of things. Not really for anyone else, but primarily for herself, an explanation and a journey, almost a jour*nal* in some ways. Unlike many hip-hop albums being released, one of its most important factors was integrity, something that had been there a great deal in the old soul records, but which had become somewhat blanded out in the face of so much commercial pressure. At the same time, hip-hop would be an important element; after all, Lauryn had said she wouldn't have wanted to be born into a world where hip-hop didn't exist. It had helped shape her, and it was a music she'd been involved in, and knew probably more intimately than any other.

She also understood that the story she was telling, while personal, was actually the story of millions of black woman—and women in general—in America. Talking about it, bringing it all into the open, would be empowering, not only for Lauryn herself, but for women everywhere, and that was important, although it wasn't quite a prime mover behind the record.

". . . This is just one woman's story," she added. "What I'm saying shouldn't be confused with me telling *anybody* how they should live their life." Experience, the people telling her to leave the Fugees, not to have a baby, had taught her that much. You had to make your own decisions, walk your own path, and be strong every single moment. Someone as recognized as jazz singer Nina Simone had said to Lauryn, "I don't think a woman can have a family and be in the music business." But Lauryn had never accepted that as right for her. She'd talked the talk, and she'd walk the walk. Now she was describing what she'd gone through on the way. "It's really our passage into adulthood when we leave that place of idealism and naivete." These were lessons she hadn't learned at Columbia—the lessons of life, not academia.

eight

How well did it all work? The simple answer was that it succeeded on every level.

"I was thinking that hip-hop and R&B as we now know them aren't as personal and intimate as the music I want to make—a lot of it is very braggadocious and cool," she said. "I was nervous that people weren't going to be able to relate, or would think I'm a Martian."

Instead, they responded as if *The Miseducation of Lauryn Hill* was something of a gift to modern music. In *Entertainment Weekly*, David Browne described it as "easily flowing from singing to rapping, evoking the past while forging a future of her own, Hill has made an album of often-astonishing power, strength, and feeling." He concluded that "On the Fugees' *The Score*, Hill rapped of having 'inner visions like Stevie.' At the time, the line seemed like hollow bluster from a trio that leaned so heavily on the past. But on *The Miseducation of Lauryn Hill*, she's begun to deliver on that boast, and it truly is the sweetest thing.''

People found it ''an exhilarating mix of warmly expressive singing, hip-hop and reggae flavored-rhythms and Hill's often no-nonsense lyrics,'' saying ''she raises the bar for intelligent, introspective pop.''

Allison Samuels in *Newsweek* noted that the album was filled with the tensions of her life, saying that she'd ''made an entire album to let us know just how she feels about all this. Black female rage has never sounded as good . . .'' giving ''the listeners an up-close-and-personal look at a black woman who feels used and abused,'' although ''at her best, Hill opens her heart with wondrous results.''

The Source called her ''the flyest MC ever,'' and no less a paper than *The New York Times* hailed her work on the record as ''visionary.'' You couldn't ask for better accolades.

And when it was released in August 1998, album buyers seemed to agree wholeheartedly. *The Miseducation of Lauryn Hill* broke the record for first-week sales by a female artist, according to Soundscan, which monitored retail sales. And that meant by *any* female artist, including Madonna, Whitney, Mariah, even Celine Dion. With 422,624 copies of the record vanishing out of stores in the first week, it debuted on the *Billboard* album chart at Number One. Prior to this, the highest figure for sales ever in the first week had been for Madonna's *Ray of Light*, which had sold 371,000 copies in March 1998 (but still only debuted at #2, beneath *Titanic*). It put Lauryn in an elite group, with Madonna, Janet Jackson, Celine Dion, and the late Selena, as the only women to have sold more than 300,000 copies of an album in the first week of release.

For a woman who was only twenty-two when she wrote and recorded it all, and a new mother to boot, it really was an astonishing piece of work. It picked up where the Fugees had left off on *The Score*, and took the process two steps further. This time, though, the vision was personal, and Lauryn didn't have to compromise the things she wanted to do to accommodate the ideas of Clef and Pras. And, as predicted, it showed that she had been much more than just the singer in that band, as some had dismissed her. Instead, here was someone with real creative power.

The album essentially defined itself with the introduction, a home room, with a teacher taking attendance. Only Lauryn Hill was missing from the class, attending to her own miseducation.

"Lost Ones" was a manifesto, a hard, syncopated drumbeat. Recorded in Jamaica, it brought together musical elements of hip-hop and reggae. There was scratching, guitar, some rapping—in a definitely Jamaican style, and some lovely, sweet singing on the chorus. You had to be good to other people, treat them right, because under the law of karma, all your misdeeds would return to you. And even if you escaped justice in this life, who knew what was waiting in the next one? In a lot of ways, it excoriated men, those who would fall to temptation too easily, unlike women, who had the new lives of their babies to protect and fight for. If you gained the world and lost your soul, was it worth the price? Lauryn was asking questions, not offering the answers—those all lay within, where each individual could find them. In that regard, by her definition it was a gospel track, even if there was no gospel sound on it. Lyrically, it could also be interpreted— and was, by some—as a dig at both Pras and Clef, who seemed to have fallen into the trap of stardom for its own sake. Was that how Lauryn meant it, though? She wasn't saying. You could read into it what you wanted.

Indeed, the sound was completely individual, cleaner than anything the Fugees had done, more controlled. There was nothing more than a hint of reggae, although the spring of the instruments had a feel that American musicians seemed unable to attain. As a lead-off, a statement of purpose, it stood proud and tall, an indication of what was to come on the record. It all ended with the teacher spelling L-O-V-E on the blackboard and asking his class for the titles of songs and movies about love.

"Ex-Factor" had even been originally intended for this album, Lauryn said. Instead, it had been written for another singer, in a higher key. But when she'd finished it, she saw how it fit perfectly into the pattern she was creating, and kept it for her own. A product both of Kingston and New York. Again, the subject was men, but this time how men often acted in relationships, so close one minute, so distant the next, the passive-aggressive behavior that seemed drilled into them from birth, desiring, then rejecting. And women weren't exactly blameless, either. They kept letting the men who'd mistreated them back into their lives. What they both needed was just to walk away from an untenable situation. But of course, neither of them could, hanging on in the very grim and pointless hope that it would all work out. It was autobiography, but it was more than that. It echoed universal sentiments of the problems between the sexes, the pains and scars that everyone felt.

Musically it "replayed elements" from the standard "Can It All Be So Simple," sounding

sophisticated and soulful, somewhat reminiscent of the style of the late Minnie Ripperton,
although there was no way Lauryn could try to
reproduce Minnie's high range. Not that there
was any need; the soul was in the delivery of
her singing, spoken word echoing her vocal
line, the deep, rich sound of the timpani lending a heavy accent to the percussion line. The
hook came straight from sixties soul—it would
have been to imagine someone like Ann Peebles or Aretha singing it, Lauryn's way of in-
directly paying homage to her influences, while
keeping true to her own style. Her own massed
background vocals provided a thick cushion for
her head in the old skool fashion of R&B, and
the additional production of Vada Nobles offered the kind of sheen that the song virtually
demanded. As she'd originally written it, the
song had a guitar solo on the fade, and it was
still there—maybe not as screaming as she'd
envisioned it, but what Johari Newton offered
was perfect for the track.

From there it moved into what was perhaps
the most heartfelt track of the whole record,
the one she'd written for her baby, "To Zion."
Inevitably, since this was *her* story, there was
a mention of those who'd suggest she abort the
baby, and of the decision she'd made to carry
him. But that was only part of the tale. It was
a love song, albeit not one of the standard kind,

a love song to the life she held, that depended on her and loved her unconditionally. However, there was also another layer of meaning, the Biblical Zion, which was often referenced in both the Baptist church and Rastafarianism. That most definitely made this a gospel song.

There was the hip-hop feel to the live drums, all overlaid by the acoustic and electric guitar work of Carlos Santana, fluid and sympathetic, weaving in and out of the vocal line. The harp accented the second verse in a heavenly style, behind Lauryn's sing-speak that broke into true gospel fashion with the background vocals on the chorus, then on the vocal fade. The massed talents of Sabrina Johnston, Lenesha Randolph, Earl Robinson, Andrea Simmons, Kenny Bobien, and Eddie Stockley worked, while Lauryn's voice ''testified'' over the top. The song used elements of Gimble and Fox's soul classic ''And the Feeling's Good'' to very full effect in the melody line.

It all built beautifully to the climax, where Lauryn reached for, and held, a note that seemed as if it should have been way out of her range. Still, it was perfectly in keeping with the spirit of the song that she should achieve it. The co-production by Che Guevara managed both a silky finish and a nubby rawness, which the song needed.

''When I heard the song, it broke me up,''

Santana said. "... Your heart says, 'Go this way,' so you go that way. It takes a lot of courage to do that." The album, he thought, was "proving to the world that quality and quantity can dance together."

The lyrics on the album bared Lauryn's soul, but "I really don't know any better," she explained. "If you're trying to be an artist, the idea is to grow. I tried to be creative and not do the same thing, but there are always people who are going to be skeptical ... It's all right, though, because I think adversity makes you push and fight that much more ... I guess I'm not afraid of a little struggle."

And the struggle, specifically between black men and women, was highlighted on the next track, "Doo Wop (That Thing)" which would also go on to become a Number One single, a staple on radio and television throughout the fall. It was introduced by more of the classroom interludes, where the teacher asked the kids to define love, and if any of the students had ever been in love.

The crux of the song was respect for each other, and respect for oneself, valuing oneself as more than a sex object.

It came on like a short trip through black music, from the doo-wop harmonies that brought it in, through the soul horns, into the hip-hop of the nineties, with even some DJ work on the turntables, before exploding into a true R&B chorus.

The verses addressed each sex: first, the women, telling them not to give it up too easily, to value their bodies, their sex, and their love, and not to fall for some guy who just wanted to sleep with them, and then was never heard from again. Nor should they just give in to trends like hair weaves and long fake nails; these were only surface, and you needed to go deeper than that. At the same time, Lauryn pointed out, she was only human, and she'd let herself be used by men before.

That was compassionate. With the men she was less sparing, deriding those who simply tried to live up to an image of gangsta wannabes with their cars and Timberland boots, the ones who wanted to pack a gun, buying champagne for the girls when in fact they were still living with their mothers, and going to court when they failed to pay the child support for the kids they'd fathered. They weren't men, she pointed out, but boys dressed up in adult clothing, unable to face up to the responsibilities that come with maturity.

It was the chorus that was the real hook, soulful, gorgeous, the making of a connection between the Southern soul from Memphis and Muscle Shoals—the horn line even sounded like it had been taken from something made in

Memphis—and Kingston, where it was recorded; real Jamaican music, as it had developed, had its roots in American R&B.

The song showed the way Lauryn could develop her musical ideas, and blend elements of past and present in a delightfully fresh brew that appealed to a wide range of people in terms of the music, and specifically to black women in terms of her lyrics. You could sing along with the chorus and be delighted with the introduction and leave the rest, or you could pay attention to the words and be educated. The choice was yours. Either way, the music was irresistible, and for many, that was all that mattered in making it a hit single— which it just deserved to be.

''Superstar'' was seen by many as a poke at her Fugees colleagues, and maybe it was. Or it could easily have been directed at so many in hip-hop who simply recycled the past to make new hits, without adding any creativity of their own into the mix. Still, Lauryn pointed out, those who lived the superstar life could also fall by it, because there was simply no substitute for true creativity. Those who had it, worked; those who didn't were simply fronting. It was also short autobiography, about why she'd started in music in the first place: not to be a star, but simply to say her piece.

That Lauryn would utilize melodic elements

(and a line) from the Doors' rock classic "Light My Fire" showed not only the range of her musical tastes, but also a small tribute to creativity, since the Doors had been widely acknowledged as one of the most creative bands of the late 1960s.

The classroom introduction to the song highlighted the difference between love and being in love, an important distinction. When you're in love with someone or something, what's on the surface doesn't matter; it's what's underneath that's important, and this was reflected in the lyrics of the song. Again Lauryn was offering her sing-speak, with singing behind, intertwining R&B, hip-hop, and soul in her very distinctive way. The backing, highlighting the harpsichord and harp, offered a light juxtaposition to the harshness of the words (and Lauryn herself played guitar on the track, although it was hidden in the mix). And when she dropped her rhymes in the middle section, she was as hard as anyone from the 'hood. This time it wasn't all her own work, though, as James Poyser contributed to the music, and Johari Newton helped out with the lyrics.

By Lauryn's definition, "Final Hour" was also a gospel song, inasmuch as it cautioned against the hedonism of life, taking too much delight in the pleasures of life, rather than thinking ahead to that final hour when you have to face your maker. At the same time, Lauryn wasn't above giving herself a bit of a big up in the first verse, and it was justified, because unlike so many other rappers, she was simply telling the truth, rather than trying to be grandiose and bragging. In the third verse there were Biblical allusions, some obvious, others implied (like the rich man not getting into Heaven). Things, she felt, would change, and the meek really would inherit the earth. Always, whoever you were, you had to think ahead to the title of the final hour. Rappers weren't immune, either; you could drop your rhymes, but that meant nothing if you didn't lead a good life.

It was a jazzy vibe, with a lovely flute solo bringing in the rhymes, Lauryn truly hard on the mic, harder than she'd even been, even with the Fugees. The chorus used her voice singing in the background, punctuated by some live brass. Her own voice, double-tracked, emphasized some phrases and words.

The spirit was right, and it was a wonderful change to hear someone realizing that there was life beyond the present, that you needed to think of more than a new car or more expensive jewelry, and it was a definite warning to those who lived their lives that way. They could if they wanted, but in the end they'd pay the price. Lauryn, meanwhile, would follow a more spiritual path. She'd still enjoy her life, and the success it had given her, but it couldn't be the be-all and end-all for her. From the hip-hop it took off into jazz, Lauryn singing like a younger Cassandra Wilson over the instuments.

"When It Hurts So Bad" was that perfect mix of Jamaica and old-skool soul music. The drum fill that brought in the vocals couldn't have come from anywhere but Jamaica, where part of the track had been recorded.

It was exquisitely personal in its lyrics, but at the same time totally universal, about the pain of romance, both as it progressed and as it ended. There was the heartbreak that came with the finish, the anguish in the heart. Lauryn was forced to question whether it was really love she was feeling, though, this desire to relinquish her power as a woman, a person, an individual, for someone else. But sometimes the thing you needed would turn out right—not often, however. It had obviously been written about a specific time in her life, part of the journey from innocence to experience: her miseducation, as she very aptly called it, another of life's hard lessons in reality, the things they didn't teach you in school.

The bass and drums came straight outta Kingston, but the rest was pure American soul music, overlaid with a modern R&B feel.

There was a sweetness to it all, courtesy of the harp, that made a contrast to the basic sadness of the song. It also showed how much Lauryn had developed as a vocalist since "Killing Me Softly With His Song," where her singing seemed raw and essentially unformed in comparison. This was a woman who could handle jazz as easily as she could do anything else, who'd quietly become a top-notch singer. The real turning point, of course, had been "The Sweetest Thing," which had marked her as someone fulfilling the promise she'd shown with the Fugees. But this was somene who'd served her apprenticeship and come out the other side, both musically and emotionally.

It faded out into the classroom again, once more discussing love, before going into the song that was the logical successor to "When It Hurts So Bad," "I Used to Love Him," where R&B diva Mary J. Blige lent her talents to the track. "She sings from the heart," Lauryn said of her friend, and it was quite true here. This was the aftermath of the last situation, a woman who's not only come to terms with the fact that romance has ended, but has gotten over it, and can look back dispassionately and berate herself for what she did. Not so much for being in love, but for losing control, and putting her lover ahead of God in her life, as Lauryn admitted she had done. The analogy she made was with drug addiction, and it was a good one; what she needed was her fix of her man, and she was going to get it, no matter what. In the end, giving herself back to God left her feeling whole again, complete.

Lauryn and Mary shared the lead vocals, with nine massed background singers behind them. This was completely modern R&B, but with a remarkably jazzy edge behind the strong, kickin' hip-hop beat, propelled by an odd little keyboard beat, much of the melody coming, unusually enough, from the background vocals, as the two singers traded off lines with each other.

It made for a strange track, but one that was curiously addictive, the keyboard acting as a hook (Lauryn had never lost her pop smarts) with a leaning toward blues, the choir of voices hinting at gospel (as was only right for the subject matter of redemption). The singers pushed each other further and higher, without ever losing control of the song: *that* was kept on a tight rein. All in all, it stood out as a small masterpiece, both of writing and arranging, tricky to pull off successfully, but in the end as smooth as silk.

"Forgive Them Father" was Lauryn's interpretation of Bob Marley's "Concrete Jungle." It was a warning song, to watch out for others with their own hidden agendas, and the way they could use someone who was naive, suck them dry and then cast them aside. It went beyond the personal to the resolutely political, wondering why so many people always wanted more, whether it be power, money, or whatever. Or why the black race had always been willing to settle for slightly less than others, because the others wanted to be on top. At the same time, like the Lord's Prayer, the song asked God to forgive those wrongdoers, because no one was innately evil, even if they stabbed you in the back and tried to climb over the bodies. Maybe falseness was part of human nature, but it was something she'd been working all her life to avoid in herself.

As befitted the song's Jamaican roots, some of it was sung in patois, the common language of Jamaica, which helped make the song more universal.

Of course, it couldn't have been recorded anywhere but Kingston, with a strong Jamaican cast, including Bob's son, Julian, on guitar. There was no substitute for the real feel of people who'd grown up playing reggae. But it was a slicker, more Americanized version, behind Lauryn's decidedly R&B vocals. The Fugees had pioneered the mix of reggae and hip-hop, but it had never sounded as good as this, the rhythm forming a solid backdrop for the rhymes Lauryn dropped in the middle of the song, dubbing out the horns behind her voice to add another dimension to the sound. It was soulful, and, with its lyrical gospel motif, added to the continuum of black music.

The idea of asking God for forgiveness flowed quite naturally from the previous track; there was a logical progression to the tracks, a narrative of a sort. And the idea of compassion fit perfectly with the spirituality of Bob Marley, who had been the song's musical inspiration.

Then it was back to the classroom to talk more about love, and a boy realizing it was important to consider what a girl was thinking and feeling, which led into Lauryn's reminiscence of her childhood in "Every Ghetto, Every City." Everyone has memories like these, even if they aren't the same ones—the good times, the little things that make each childhood special. This was a journey back, both lyrically and musically, with a clavinet sound that came straight out of Stevie Wonder (who'd been one of her earliest musical idols), recalling "Living for the City" in particular, which was only right, given that this was a very urban hymn, and replaying elements of two songs from the eighties, "Tony Poem" and Steve Hurley's early house music classic, "Jack Your Body," both of which had been part of Lauryn's adolescence and carried her back to that time.

It was those times that had helped shape Lauryn into who she was today, and she advised people never to forget their youth, to keep the good times in their hearts, close to the surface, not just as old memories, but as part of the fabric of every human being.

It was funky—a word that rarely truly applied to music in the nineties—propelled not so much by the drum machine, but by the playground rhythms of hand-claps. It was vocally loose, a warm, fond look backwards, and as infectious as any track Stevie Wonder had recorded. But it couldn't be totally retro: there was a little scratching in there too, but that had also been a part of Lauryn's upbringing.

After that, the kids were talking about love again, and how, when you love, you want to be loved, too. And good love was the subject of Lauryn's duet with D'Angelo on ''Nothing Even Matters,'' which almost certainly seemed to be about her relationship with Rohan Marley, the excellent relationship that followed the terrible one before it. Lauryn had long loved the old soul duos, Marvin Gaye and Tammi Terrell, Roberta Flack and Donny Hathaway, and had aspired to do one of her own. D'Angelo was a natural fit for that, she said because ''We have a similar philosophy . . . I wanted it to be about what it's like when your back starts to tingle and your stomach feels funny.''

This definitely evoked that special feeling, but it was in a more positive way than her last romance. The singer was in love, but she'd learned from her experiences. The outside world might not matter, and she was head over heels, but this was the real thing, not the illusions she'd gone through before, and she understood the difference.

It was a gorgeous, sexy slow jam, one that slinked along, with finger clicks as its rhythm, D'Angelo being one of the players on electric piano, the guitar of former Wailer Al Anderson sliding in and out of the mix, fat chords on the Hammond organ cushioning the sound. The two voices played perfectly off each other, certainly more Roberta and Donny than Marvin and Tammi in the softness and sheer sensuality of the track, and it brought back memories of the older Quiet Storm style of soul music.

And from nothing mattering at all (except love), the natural follow-up was that ''Everything is Everything.'' This was about change, that change happens, and that it can be good as well as bad. Mixing scratching strings over a heavy rhythm, it was very different in its sound, an original mix of elements.

Change could take many forms. The idealism of youth faded as adulthood set in and the rules changed. But if we sowed our seeds when we were young, then maybe in maturity they would grow, and we would become the people we could be—positive instead of negative. Accepting change, that things grew, that things moved on, was perhaps life's major lesson, and one that Lauryn had learned, at her cost (with some additional lyrical help from Johari Newton).

This wasn't R&B; it wasn't hip-hop, even if it had a rap. Nor was it soul music. It was as if Lauryn had invented something new from everything that had gone before, and taken it two steps further. It was possibly the most revolutionary piece on the entire record, at least musically, a possible new direction for hip-hop.

The title track, "The Miseducation of Lauryn Hill," tied it all together. The education everyone is given might give them some facts, but it doesn't prepare them for dealing with life in the world. Everyone has unrealistic expectations put on them, but you can't be that, because that's not *you*. Everyone has his or her own destiny, and that is what you have to go for; otherwise it becomes a wasted life. And the only way to find out who you are is to look inside, to examine yourself, and take strength from God to do it, even if it's not easy. The past shapes us, but the future can be our own.

The fake vinyl scratches on the track marked it as being in an older style, the Hammond organ, piano, and strings melding gorgeously to form a jazzy backdrop for Lauryn's mellifluous voice. Tejumold Newton gave additional musical contribution, to an arrangement that had its roots in the Baptist church, but moved far beyond that. It was spare, notable for no drums or percussion, but still very rich, particularly Loris Holland's superb organ playing that moved all through the cut.

Anyone who didn't eject the album after the last advertised cut got a special treat of the Refugee Camp and Conspiracy Theory updating an oldie, ''Can't Take My Eyes Off You'' (best known as a solo hit for Four Seasons frontman Frankie Valli in 1967). In this case, Refugee Camp was Lauryn alone, updating the song in much the same way the Fugees had recut ''Killing Me Softly With His Song.'' There was no doubt it was a lovely melody, and very soulful, although it initially seemed like a curious choice. But this was for fun, nothing too serious. It brought the song into the hip-hop era, with a heavy accent on the beat, the bass accenting the beat, while the organ kept the chords shimmering. It was played as straight as the Roberta Flack remake, Lauryn singing her heart out, the background vocals a strong cushion on the chorus. Of course, it didn't fit into the song cycle that made up the album; there was no room for a straight cover there; but its spirit was right, and it gave L a chance to exercise her vocal chops, both as background and lead singer, a little rawer than she was on her own material, but nonetheless enjoyable.

And from there, the album went into yet another hidden track—a prayer that was sung, almost a hymn, a prayer to God, to Zion, to Rohan, over a thick beat, and fingerpicked guitar chords. It was one of the most heartfelt and naked songs on the record, with a real gospel feel finessed through some fifties harmonies, the harmony vocals providing the real melodic accompaniment to Lauryn's lead. It was a gentle, and very apt, note on which to end the record.

At seventy-seven-and-a-half minutes, *The Miseducation of Lauryn Hill* wasn't a short record. But it covered a lot of ground, musically and emotionally. It needed the time and the space, and every second was well used.

nine

The album was incredibly successful, staying at the top of the charts for four weeks, and sticking around the top twenty of the *Billboard* album listings well into 1999 (after the announcement of the Grammy nominations, of which Lauryn received ten, on January 5, the album climbed the charts again), and selling more than three million copies. It was also a massive hit in a number of countries, including Britain and Japan, where it went to Number One and achieved platinum status.

That would have been achievement enough for something that was as adventurous and artistic as this. But Lauryn went one better. As well as the Number One album in America, she also had the Number One single, as ''Doo Wop (That Thing)'' hit the top of the *Billboard* Hot 100. The CD single contained five tracks, the radio edit of ''Doo Wop (That Thing),'' the album version and a remix of ''Lost Ones,'' and instrumental and *a capella* versions of "Doo Wop (That Thing)," making it an essential package for fans and even casual listeners. The video, showing Lauryn looking like a sixties Motown girl (that was a wig, not a hair weave) was all over BET, MTV, The Box, and VH-1; you could hardly turn around without seeing it.

But the video and some interviews prior to the release of *The Miseducation of Lauryn Hill* were the extent of the publicity Lauryn was doing. There would be no immediate tour, and no television appearances. In the event, the record didn't need it, but there was a strong reason behind it all: Lauryn was pregnant again, with her second child. She'd conceived in February, and the baby was due early in December. With Zion just over a year old, it made sense to have another quickly, to keep him company and grow up with him. And it indicated that Lauryn's priority was her family, more than her record. She wanted to express all sides of herself. This time there was no doubt that Rohan Marley was the father. Their relationship had continued happily and quietly, out of the spotlight.

"My relationship isn't a publicity stunt," Lauryn said. "We don't do things to get in the paper. We just live." Although they were as good as married now, they had plans to make it all official sometime in the near future, although the event would be kept very private, and away from the media. And it seemed likely that Lauryn would have no difficulty doing that; so far she'd separated her personal and professional lives fiercely, and in a manner that had been most effective. In all likelihood, the marriage wouldn't even be announced until the ceremony was over. And even in the wake of this new success, the family would live just as they had. Lauryn's attachment to the house in South Orange and the neighborhood around it was strong. She wasn't going to leave that, not now. Her children would be able to grow up as she had, and enjoy the same, normal kind of upbringing.

"People suggest home or private school, but I don't want to alienate my son," she explained. "I want him to be exposed to everything. I want him to go abroad, to see that the world is a lot bigger than five blocks. I want him to have a regular childhood."

And on November 12, 1998, that expanded from just "him." In a New York City hospital, Lauryn gave birth to Selah Louise Marley (weight seven pounds, twelve ounces). She'd wanted a girl this time, and her wish was answered. Of course, the birth meant that she wasn't going to be doing anything other than looking after her children for the next few weeks. But even her low personal profile didn't keep her out of the press between then and the end of the year.

It was time for magazines and writers to start naming their albums of the year. *The Miseducation of Lauryn Hill* had received rave reviews on its release, but it was only one of thousands of records to appear during 1998. However, it had obviously made an impression on a lot of critics, to judge by the issues that hit the newsstands in the last couple of weeks of the year.

Entertainment Weekly named Lauryn Entertainer of the Year. *Time* heralded *Miseducation* as its Album of the Year, as did the very prestigious *New York Times*. *USA Today* voted it Best R&B Album of 1998. In *Spin*, Lauryn was Artist of the Year, as she was in *Details*. In the *Rolling Stone* Music Awards, Lauryn won in several categories. "Doo Wop (That Thing)" was the Best Single of the Year, *The Miseducation of Lauryn Hill* was named Best Album, she was Best R&B Artist, and just to round it all off, also Best Female Artist, while in the readers' poll in the magazine, she was voted Best R&B Artist.

While these offered a veritable shelf-full of awards, they were nothing more than the beginning. At the annual *Billboard* Music Awards, *The Miseducation of Lauryn Hill* won for R&B Album of the Year, while at the twentieth *Billboard* Music Video Awards, "Doo Wop (That Thing)" walked away with Best R&B/Urban New Artist Clip.

Then, just to finish 1998 on a high note, Lauryn received a number of nominations in the thirtieth NAACP Image Awards. There were Outstanding New Artist, Outstanding Female Artist, Outstanding Album, Outstanding Music Video (not for her own song, but for her direction of Aretha's "A Rose is Still a Rose"), and finally she would be competing against herself for Outstanding Song, nominated both for "Doo Wop (That Thing)" and "A Rose is Still a Rose."

Christmas at least brought a break, a time for the family to gather in New Jersey, to coo over the new baby and her older brother, and for Lauryn to catch her breath after the mad round of awards. "Doo Wop (That Thing)" had gone gold, meaning it had sold more than half a million copies, and it probably wouldn't be too long before the album turned quadruple platinum. Life was sweet.

But a rest was what she needed, because in the new year life was going to get considerably busier. While Lauryn hadn't toured behind the record, that was simply because pregnancy hadn't allowed it. Now, having delivered, she was getting back in shape, and working on her voice to begin performing live again. It had always been her intention to take *The Miseducation of Lauryn Hill* on the road, and her management went ahead and began setting up dates. Nor would it be anything as simple as Lauryn onstage performing to a DAT backing tape. This would be a full-on show, with a complete live band and a DJ. She'd learned in the Fugees that it was important to make it real, to present the songs as they should be presented. It would be rawer than the record, but that was fine. It would be *her* vision transferred to the stage.

That would mean intense rehearsals with a bunch of musicians, familiarizing them with the material, figuring out arrangements that would work on the road (as opposed to just in the studio), and letting the songs grow, develop, and change a little. It wasn't in Lauryn's nature to keep things static, and there was certainly no artistic satisfaction in doing everything by rote, night after night. There had to be an edge, an element of danger, of walking a highwire without a safety net, to keep it exciting.

Lauryn's popularity was immense in Japan, who had taken to her and her album in a huge way. So that was where the tour would begin, and as soon as the dates were announced, for massive stadiums and halls, the tickets sold out. It would start on January 21 at Budokan in Tokyo, where she'd play again the following night, before moving on to another venue in Tokyo on the twenty-third, and finally in Osaka on the twenty-fifth. It was short, just four dates, but it would give the band a chance to shake down, and work out the musical problems that inevitably happened at the beginning of any big tour. And, obviously, with two young children at home, Lauryn had no desire to be gone from New Jersey from extended periods of time. After the Japanese dates there'd be a week and a half to regroup in America, a chance to see Rohan, Zion and Selah, as well as refine arrangements with the band, before flying into London on February 5 to perform a one-off show at the Brixton Academy (where the Fugees had triumphed in 1996, commemorated by the live version of "Killing Me Softly With His Song" on *Bootleg Versions*). It was a long way to travel for a single show, but it was both a thank-you to the fans, and a way of testing the waters for a possible European tour later in the year.

Before any of that could begin, however, it was time for another awards ceremony, and on January 11, on ABC television, the twenty-sixth annual American Music Awards took place. Perhaps it was inevitable, but Lauryn walked away with the trophy for Favorite New

Soul/R&B Artist. It made a nice addition to all the others she'd been winning recently.

Six days before that, she'd received what had to be a massive boost to her confidence before the tour. On January 5, the nominations for the Grammy Awards had taken place. Given the way things had been going, it seemed certain that Lauryn would receive a couple. What happened, though, flabbergasted everyone. She received *ten* separate nominations, a truly staggering figure, and one that had rarely been achieved before. It was a sign that the committee behind the Grammy Awards rated her work as both a commercial and artistic success, and a real acknowledgment of Lauryn's talents.

Of course, nominations didn't *always* translate into awards, as Mariah Carey had found a few years before. But simply to be nominated was an honor, especially when there was also a call from the show's presenters asking Lauryn to perform, which she agreed to do, singing her most recent single, ''Ex-Factor,'' which had just appeared in January.

She'd been nominated for Album of the Year (for *The Miseducation of Lauryn Hill*), Best New Artist, Best Female Pop Vocal Performance (for ''Can't Take My Eyes Off You,'' one of the hidden tracks on her album), Best Female R&B Vocal Performance (for

"Doo Wop (That Thing),") Best R&B Performance by a Duo or Group with Vocal (for "Nothing Even Matters," her collaboration with D'Angelo), Best R&B Song ("Doo Wop (That Thing),") Best R&B Album, Best Rap Solo Performance (for "Lost Ones"), and Best R&B Song (for "A Rose is Still a Rose," her composition for Aretha). She'd also been nominated twice in the Producer of the Year, non-classical, category, both for *The Miseducation of Lauryn Hill* and "A Rose is Still a Rose."

That was a pretty impressive haul of nominations, particularly since two of them were for album tracks, not even singles, showing just the kind of esteem in which she was held. Certainly Lauryn herself was taken aback by it all, and issued a statement saying "I'd like to thank everyone who supported this album. I think it is a strong statement, in these days, that I can make an album completely from my soul and without compromise and be acknowledged for it. Praise God."

What, in real terms, did all the nominations mean? Well, they sent her album scurrying back up the chart. People who'd shown little or no interest in it before were suddenly aware that it was good and hurried out to buy it (although that would be nothing compared to the sales boost if it won Album of the Year). And it continued the spotlight focus on her as an artist, which hadn't really stopped since the record appeared in August. For someone who'd kept such a low profile, and who'd been more concerned with impending and then new motherhood, rather than career, she'd been the subject of more articles than an artist who wanted publicity.

Still, it all helped set the stage for what would be a fairly extensive American concert tour. By the time Lauryn opened in Detroit on February 18, the band would be tight from their Japanese shows, the audience would be full of expectations, and it all promised to be quite rousing. Detroit would be followed by Chicago on the twenty-first, then St. Louis the day after, before a four-day break, ostensibly for the Grammy Awards, but also giving Lauryn a chance to go home and see her babies. Then it would resume on the twenty-sixth in Kansas City, before heading on to Denver the following night. After that there'd be another short break, until March 2, when the tour would pick up in Oakland, then San Francisco, after which everyone would head down the coast for two shows in Universal City on the fifth and sixth, before playing the gambling capital of America, Las Vegas, on the seventh.

Then it was Dallas on March 10, Houston on the eleventh, and Atlanta on the thirteenth, followed by a week's break, interrupted only

by a show in Washington, D.C. on the six-
teenth, once again giving Lauryn time to see
her family and recharge her batteries; after all,
she'd just given birth in November, which
meant that she'd still be subject to some post-
partum exhaustion. The tour's final leg started
in Cleveland on March 21, then headed to New
York for two dates at Madison Square Garden
on the twenty-third and twenty-fourth. After
another break, it was Upper Darby, PA on the
twenty-eighth, Boston on the thirty-first, and
everything wound up with what was essentially
a homecoming in Newark on April 1.

It wasn't an exhaustive schedule, nothing
compared to the touring the Fugees did in
1996, but that was the point. Lauryn might
have plenty of energy, but she still wasn't back
to full physical strength, and able to endure
long periods on the road. Nor did she want to.
She had strong memories of that '96 tour and
how it had affected her, and had no desire to
repeat that. Touring was its own reality, insu-
lated from everyday life. If you spent too much
time on the road (and in '96 the Fugees had
done forty-two dates in forty-two nights) it
skewed your perceptions of the world, and that
was one thing she definitely didn't want. With
a family, her priorities needed to be very clear;
they came ahead of everything else. Even with
her mother and Rohan at home to look after

the kids, they were still *her* kids, growing and changing every single day, and she didn't want to miss out on that. So the tour became a balancing act, a compromise. She loved to perform, and was eager to play this material live, but not at the expense of her family.

There was the possibility of more dates being added (and some of those listed being changed), but it was unlikely that Lauryn would be willing to make the tour more grueling and draining. She'd come to know that there was much more to life than a career.

Even as she hit Japan, there were new award nominations coming in, and it seemed as if they would never stop. In the Brits, Britain's answer to the Grammy Awards, Lauryn had been nominated as Best International Female Solo Artist, up against Sheryl Crow, Natalie Imbruglia, Madonna, and Alanis Morrissette—some pretty high-flying company.

In the final event, though, it didn't really matter whether she won another award or not. It was fine to be nominated, and in itself that was a huge victory, because it meant she'd won acceptance on her own terms. *The Miseducation of Lauryn Hill* had been the record *she* wanted to make, and every step of it had been done her way, without any sort of compromise. It built on everything she'd learned and experienced, and stood as a work of art.

That others had got it and bought it had almost been a bonus for her.

"In New York, I've had Italian cops come up to me at the Port Authority [bus station] and tell me they love the record," she recounted. "I think the world is a lot smaller than I thought [it was] growing up."

It was quite definitely a woman's record, coming from a woman's heart and a woman's,—and more specifically, a black woman's—battles, but in the way of the best art, she'd managed to touch a universal chord. It went beyond hip-hop, even beyond hip, to the emotions. You didn't have to be young to understand. Indeed, the emotions went far beyond puppy love, as the classroom interludes showed all too well; there was nothing simple about love.

Even though it hadn't sold in quite the numbers as Clef's solo album (*The Carnival* had topped five million copies in the U.S. alone), it had been much higher-profile, and all the praise Lauryn had received tended to overshadow the solo debut of the third Fugee, Pras, when he released *Ghetto Supastar* in October 1998. For all that there seemed to be little communication between the three band members (or ex-members, possibly), it was notable that on all three solo records, the others were thanked. The Fugees might no longer exist, but it seemed as if the Refugee Camp would continue.

Of the three solo albums, *Ghetto Supastar* was the lowest seller, and possibly the least visionary, musically. But Pras was no longer confining himself to music. In January, 1999, he issued his first book, also named *Ghetto Supastar*, written with journalist Kris Ex, who'd previously covered the Fugees. It was the story of Diamond, a young MC trying to put together the demo tape he knew would break him into the big time. His best friend Michael (*aka* Gage) had taken the gangsta path, down which Diamond was also treading to finance his recording. The third side of the triangle was made up by Tamara, a suburban black girl, strong-willed and intelligent, headed for college, but completely in love with Diamond.

It was enough to make one wonder if Tamara had been based, however loosely, on Lauryn. Certainly there were some superficial similarities, inasmuch as both had suburban upbringings, and both had college backgrounds. But Lauryn had more going on in her life than Tamara, whose creativity was making clothes and things out of leather for Diamond. And had Lauryn ever been utterly, completely in love with Pras? There were no indications of it in anything she'd ever said. Still, it was intriguing, even if it offered no real insights into any Fugees activities

While family and music were the focuses of her life, there was a strong possibility that Lauryn would, at some point, return to the area of her first real success—acting. In the light of everything that had happened since, it was easy to forget that she'd started out as an actress, on the stage and on the small and large screens. But directors hadn't forgotten. First there'd been the offer of the role in *Beloved* that she'd been forced to turn down because of her pregnancy. And the scripts hadn't stopped coming. She was adamant, however, that just like music, she wasn't going to do a movie just for its own sake.

"I want to treat films the same way I treat music," she explained, "and not just do it for the sake of doing it. I'd like to do something new and original." And, to that end, she formed her own production company, to find those new, original vehicles. She had been in talks with director Joel Schumacher, a major fan of hers, about starring in a screen adaptation of the musical *Dreamgirls*, at least until the studio decided not to go ahead with the idea. And there's still the possibility that she'll be in the movie sequel to the very popular *Mission: Impossible*.

It seems to be less a case of whether she'll

show up in a film, but *when* she'll be in one. And Schumacher, for one, is convinced that she's a born star, although the idea of film stardom probably appeals to Lauryn about as much as music stardom—in other words, not at all. It's the quality of the project, what you can put into it, and the satisfaction you can derive from it that are the important factors to her. Anything else is, at best, secondary. But at the same time, it would be a great loss if Lauryn chose to ignore one of her talents, and it seems certain that, once she has time, she'll fully rediscover that strand of herself.

It seems to be an unwritten rule of sorts that there can never be success without problems, and that has proven to be the case for Lauryn, as for other people in the past. Just before Christmas 1998, some of the musicians who'd worked on *The Miseducation of Lauryn Hill* filed suit in U.S. District Court in Newark, N.J. against both Lauryn and the record label, claiming that they deserved a share of the songwriting or production credit on thirteen of the record's fourteen listed tracks. In turn, that meant part of the profits generated by the record sales.

The musicians, Vada Nobles, Rasheem ''Kilo'' Pugh, and Johari and Tejumold Newton, who went collectively under the name

New Ark, claimed to be the primary songwriters on "Nothing Really Matters" and "Everything is Everything," and major contributors on six other songs, as well as having partial or full production credit on five tracks. On top of that, they said they'd made large and uncredited production contributions to Aretha's "A Rose is Still a Rose."

However, Nobles and the Newtons were acknowledged on the record in several instances for their "additional production" or "additional musical contribution" or "additional lyrical contribution."

In a statement issued after the suit had been filed, Lauryn said that the claims were "without any merit whatsoever," and that she felt "deeply betrayed."

And while Gordon Williams, the "Commissioner Gordon" who engineered most of the sessions for the album, wouldn't comment directly on the suit, he did say that "Lauryn is a very gifted arranger, producer and writer, as well as a vocalist; she's the whole package . . . It's definitely her vision."

According to the suit, Pugh had known Lauryn for four years when she invited New Ark to help on the record. They said she made verbal assurances that they would be credited and paid for their contributions, even though they never were given that in writing, but that Lauryn backed off from her promises as the album was completed. Instead, people working with Hill arranged a publishing deal for New Ark with Sony/ATV (the same publisher who'd handled Hill's material on the record), with a $100,000 advance.

The dispute between Lauryn and New Ark had actually been the subject of discussions between their respective lawyers for a few months, but when no settlement could be reached, New Ark finally filed suit in December.

What did it all mean? If Lauryn won, then she would be vindicated as the person credited for the writing, production, and arranging on the album (the executive production credit was solely hers), and that she'd been fair with the others, who'd regarded working with her as a major break.

If the decision went against her, then she'd lose a lot of the credibility that had come her way with the record. She and others had gone to great pains to portray this as completely her record, and if it was found not to be so, it might have an effect on her standing within the industry. However, until the case was heard, nothing could be decided either way, and the National Academy of Recording Arts and Sciences, which was in charge of the Grammy

Awards, was certain it would have no effect on the Academy's voting.

But it was just one dark cloud in a sky that seemed very blue. Lauryn's appearance at the Grammy Awards and her tour would keep her profile very high indeed, and *The Miseducation of Lauryn Hill* was showing no decline in sales (on January 30 it stood at #5 on the *Billboard* charts, more than twenty-one weeks after its release). She was doing better than at any time since the Fugees had released *The Score*, and that with something that doesn't pander to the current industry standard of fast-food music, reduced to the lowest common denominator. She'd taken hip-hop to another level, just as the Fugees had done two years before, and she'd also made it possible for women to be taken seriously as creators within the industry, which was a major achievement.

For all that, she hadn't made a feminist album, just one that looked at love and life from a female point of view; a very big difference, although perhaps it was impossible to be a woman in the modern world without being something of a feminist.

And she'd brought hip-hop even further into the mainstream. Sean "Puffy" Combs might have sold millions of singles, and any number of hip-hop records jetted into the charts in high positions (to quickly fall out of sight again), but Lauryn had proved that her music had staying power. She crossed the basic barriers of race, age, and gender with songs that had *melody*. She knew the basic emotional appeal of old soul music, how that had been loved by a lot of people, including herself, and had reinvented it within a hip-hop context, which was no mean feat. So it was the baby boomers as much as the teenagers who bought *The Miseducation of Lauryn Hill*. Maybe it wasn't quite as great or important as Marvin Gaye's *What's Going On?* but then again, he wasn't just twenty-three when he made that, either. She'd made a very important first step along the way, and if she continued along the path, as it seems certain she will, then she'll very likely be making her masterpiece, a record that will live for the ages, in the next few years. That she has the ability to do it now seems beyond question. The quantum leap she made from the Fugees to her solo record spoke volumes about her rapid progress as an artist, one with a very clear-cut vision, but also one for whom the creative process is only one part of a complete life. It's the facet of her that people see, her public face, as it were, but just one piece of the whole. Maybe, by not obsessing forever on her career and her music, the huge leaps will continue to be made, and then the next record, whenever that might happen, will be as staggering as this.

But in the meantime, what about the Fugees? No one was actually admitting that they'd gone the way of the dinosaurs, but it seemed more and more likely that Lauryn, Pras, and Clef wouldn't be getting together anytime soon, even though there had been talk of a record in 1999, tentatively called *Class Reunion*.

What had happened to distance the three band members from each other had never been fully explained, but it was beginning to seem somewhat irreconcilable, which would be unfortunate. Together, they'd made some remarkable music. Even if both Clef and Lauryn had made equally excellent music individually (to be fair, Pras's record didn't seem to have the same sense of musical adventure), with what they'd learned, coming back together again could make for something that, once again, would be even greater than the sum of its parts.

Maybe, as Lauryn suggested, in a few years a channel like VH-1 would run a special on the Fugees, and the whole story would finally come out. But the band had never seemed like a mere stepping stone on the way to solo careers.

And had Lauryn moved beyond needing the Fugees? Artistically, possibly she had. Now she was no longer in the shadows and viewed as "just" the singer. She had the freedom and the scope to let her imagination run wild, and put a very personal stamp on her music, without having to compromise to fit in with the views of two other strong-willed people. Then, when that vision of hers was so widely praised, it did make the idea of joining forces with the others again seem like a step backward somehow.

If it were to happen, a Fugees reunion would initially, probably, be just for a track, maybe two, instead of sitting down with the intention of making a whole album. There's no doubt the interest would be high, particularly in the light of Lauryn's and Clef's solo success; the big question would be whether they—or anybody, for that matter—would be able to create something that lived up to the heightened expectations.

For now Lauryn has her hands full dividing her time between her family and working her own groove. To take on something extra, and something that could prove to be more frustrating than joyful, would be hard, and it seems highly unlikely. Were there to be a coming together of the Fugees in the studio in '99, it couldn't happen before the middle of the year at the earliest, after Lauryn's touring commitments have been completed.

But the simple truth, as Lauryn noted on her

album, is that change and growth happen. You accept and then mourn the past, and move on to the future, and something new. Which is exactly what she seems to have done. So it might be time, finally, to consign the Fugees to history, and fully embrace Lauryn Hill, solo artist.

conclusion

Things change: It's a rule of life. Lauryn still sits in the alcove of the brick house in South Orange, New Jersey, watching the light fade away, or spends time in the attic (now her studio) looking out of the window. The sun still shines on the projects, a few blocks away. But the magic everything had when she was a child has gone, as innocence gives way to experience. These days the house is hers. She owns the place where she once ran and played as a child, and her own children will have the joy and discovery of it all. But they'll know a different world to the one in which she grew up. Their mother is a star, whether she likes it or not, and however much she keeps the semblance of a normal life about her. They'll see the same things she did, but it will be with their own eyes, their own vision of the world and their place in it.

Still, Lauryn has provided them with a continuum, a way to keep in touch with the past, and their family history. And at the same time she's given herself some sanctuary, kept the familiar around her. It might seem an odd decision for someone who's embraced change so tightly, and who advocates the revolutionary. But then we're all a mass of contradictions. With her politics, it might seem odd, and even wrong, for Lauryn to love fashion, and to have a huge collection of shoes. After all, those things seem so fleeting, so frivolous, so *superficial*. At the same time, she's earned the right to indulge herself. They're not at the expense of anything else. She still oversees the Refugee Project, which has grown year by year. She talks the talk, and she walks the walk. If she chooses to walk it in five-inch heels and a designer dress, does it really matter?

For someone still so young, she's seen and done a lot. From the vapidity of a daytime soap opera to the sexual politics of *The Miseducation of Lauryn Hill* has been quite a journey, not just around the world, but into herself. And from the eighth grader who sang on Pras's demo tape to the mother of two headlining her own tour has also been a journey, of finding and harnessing her talent, and of being unafraid to follow her own instincts and judgment. It's not just the first step that takes courage, it's continuing along the way as your knowledge increases, and Lauryn has never shirked that—and at the same time, never forgotten her obligation to others.

Most people her age are essentially just beginning their lives. They don't yet really know themselves or what they want to do. When people like Aretha referred to Lauryn as an old soul, it was for a reason; she's wise beyond her years. That doesn't just mean she knows what to do in a recording studio, or understands how to arrange a song. It means that the light of wisdom shines through.

Wisdom, however, is always attained at a price. In Lauryn's case, its attainment has been her miseducation, as a woman, a mistreated lover, and a person of color in America. The answer is love. Not the kind of love she experienced before, but something beyond that, and that's what she found with Rohan and with her children. She came out the other side, through the tunnel and into the light, and she chronicled what she found along the way.

The Fugees were never about commerce. They made the music they wanted to make, and with *The Score*, it happily happened to be what people wanted to hear. They pushed at the boundaries of hip-hop, made it into something new, something different, taking it away from the gangsta track that was a dead end.

They were about art and politics, and hope for humanity.

Usually the pioneers never get the praise or the rewards they deserve. For the Fugees, though, both came their way, and it's also been true in Lauryn's case. Musically she's connected past, present, and future in one line, but added her own original slant on it all. And she's shown that a woman can be a very strong artist. The Lilith Fair tours of 1997 and 1998 showed the strength of women; Lauryn's work more than reflected that in hip-hop, a field where very few women have shown strength before.

She's opened the door, and others will inevitably follow. She's shown that women can be more than just the singers, they can also write, produce, direct, and arrange. They're more than capable of taking charge. As the new century approaches, with the changes it will bring, that's more important than ever. Women have the ability to lead—they have always had that—and it needs to be acknowledged. It's not been easy, and at times it was a small battle for Lauryn in the studio to get what she wanted, but the end result has been worthwhile.

As the Fugees did with *The Score*, in *The Miseducation of Lauryn Hill* she's made a record that transcends hip-hop. While that's a very important element of the sound, it goes beyond any genre or sound. It's soul, gospel, doo wop, jazz, blues, funk, reggae, a complete melting pot of black music that becomes simply great pop music. To put it very simply, it's art, not product. That alone sets it apart from most of the albums released in the quest for the consumer dollar, which simply appeal to the lowest common denominator in an attempt to make the charts and increase the bottom line. It's a record about integrity, musically and lyrically, which was why it had to be made without compromise. It's pure, undiluted and untainted because it never had an eye on the charts—and in doing that it became incredibly successful. Whether consciously or unconsciously, people can still recognize quality when it's placed in front of them and they're given a choice.

Lauryn has always had that quality that set her apart and marked her as special. The girl who acted in *As the World Turns* and made a couple of movies couldn't have done that without ambition (and support from her parents; that goes without saying). That drive has made her succeed in everything she's attempted, whether professionally or academically. While success alone might be a benchmark, it hasn't been enough for Lauryn. In fact, she's come to realize that on its own, it means nothing. If you're not making a contribution, if you're not doing something positive and uplifting, you might as well be doing nothing at all. And the most uplifting role of all, the biggest challenge of all, has been becoming a parent. To be responsible for another life outweighs everything else, to watch her children grow, and help imbue them with the right values, the same ones she received, becomes a joyful task, one that outweighs even a shelf full of awards.

It's been a long journey for someone so young, with its trials and tribulations, its dark nights and depressing, stressful times. But Lauryn has come to a place of peace and happiness. With Rohan Marley, she's found real love, love between two equals, with honest give-and-take. And from Zion and Selah there's unconditional love, the adoration of a child for a parent.

That Lauryn and Rohan will bring them up the right way is a foregone conclusion. They'll be well-rounded, not isolated in some tower of wealth. And that Lauryn will continue to create, in a number of fields, is a certainty. She's proved herself, as a singer, writer, arranger, producer, director, actress. . . . the possibilities are wide open.

The Miseducation of Lauryn Hill stood almost as a journal, a chance to assess her life, the life that had moved so rapidly, up and down like a roller coaster, to that point.

"It's sort of like being a VCR on fast-forward," she said. "You get to spots a little bit quicker than you should. There's a level of distortion. . . . The album is like regaining clarity. Just stop and pause and look at the picture for what it is."

So she took the time to look within, and brought forth the album, another child, albeit one that left the nest very quickly. And in its own way, it was every bit as difficult as giving birth, sometimes as painful, and ultimately as gladdening. A mixture of craft and inspiration, it was as unique as anything else in the universe. Like a child, it built on what it had been given by its parents, its background (in this case, Lauryn's life, and her musical expansion in the Fugees) to be something unique. She touched something deep inside herself, brought it into the open, and in her extreme, naked honesty, managed to touch plenty of others, too. That alone would have been an achievement. To do it in a way that was also musically adventurous, that took chances, was art.

What does the future hold for Lauryn Hill? The easy answer would be to say whatever she wants, and that might well be correct. With solo success and acclaim, the possibilities have become endless. Movie scripts keep arriving at her house; directors want to lunch with her. Having formed her own production company, it'll only be a matter of time before she finds a script, develops it, and quite probably has at least a supporting role in the ensuing film. Her venture directing the video for "A Rose is Still a Rose" opens plenty of doors in that direction, too. Artists, many of them female, will want her to direct their own videos. Others will be after her for songs; she's certainly proved herself as a writer. And what about record production? She's done very well at that, and will doubtless receive plenty of offers for work in that field. Finally, of course, there's the Refugee Project. Its work will continue unabated, and Lauryn will be there to offer her support, financially, spiritually, and physically, a real labor of love with its own intangible dividends.

Then there'll be the follow-up to *The Miseducation of Lauryn Hill*. While it won't be happening anytime soon, probably not before the middle of the year 2000, and quite possibly even a year after that, it will still be eagerly anticipated. In between, other artists will follow up on the paths she's cleared. Where will she go next with her music? That's a question only she can answer, and in all likelihood it's one she hasn't even begun to ask herself yet, and won't even start pondering for several months.

When her tour (which might well develop into tours) is over, she'll take time to chill, to be with her family, probably quietly marry Rohan, and readjust to the normal life she craves. Later, when she's ready, work will call again, and things will start to flow.

Right now, Lauryn could be busy every waking moment of every day. But she's been there and done that before, and knows it means nothing less than burnout. Life needs balance, and with her family, she very definitely has that. They represent her real future, her center, and her finest achievement. Everything else comes from that, the grounding they give her, and the love. Whether or not she wins all her Grammies, whether her next album is a hit or not, whether people come to see her perform, her family will always be there for her, waiting with open arms, love, and comfort. From her family will come her deepest satisfaction, and her creative impulses, the sense of being a mother, which seems to make her complete.

"Please perceive me as a mother. I've always tried to be perceived as a mother of someone—a mother of a nation, a mother of people, a mother of love."

And in that she's more than succeeded, and found total happiness. She's given, and now she's received.

discography

The Fugees—Albums

FUGEES (TRANZLATOR CREW)
Blunted On Reality
(1994—Ruffhouse / Columbia)

INTRODUCTION / NAPPY HEADS / BLUNTED IN-
TERLUDE / RECHARGE / FREESTYLE INTERLUDE
/ VOCAB / SPECIAL NEWS BULLETIN INTER-
LUDE / BOOF BAF / TEMPLE / HOW HARD IS IT? /
HARLEM CHIT CHAT INTERLUDE / SOME SEEK
STARDOM / GIGGLES / DA KID FROM HAITI
INTERLUDE / REFUGEES ON THE MIC / LIVING
LIKE THERE AIN'T NO TOMORROW / SHOUTS
OUT FROM THE BLOCK / NAPPY HEADS (REMIX)

FUGEES
The Score
(1996—Ruffhouse / Columbia)

RED INTRO / HOW MANY MICS / READY OR NOT
/ ZEALOTS / THE BEAST / FU-GEE-LA / FAMILY
BUSINESS / KILLING ME SOFTLY WITH HIS SONG
/ THE SCORE / THE MASK / COWBOYS / NO

WOMAN. NO CRY / MANIFEST / OUTRO / FU-GEE-LA (REFUGEE CAMP REMIX) / FU-GEE-LA (SLY AND ROBBIE MIX) / MISTA MISTA

Singles, EPs

BOOF BAF (1994, RUFFHOUSE / COLUMBIA)

NAPPY HEADS (REMIX) (1994, RUFFHOUSE, COLUMBIA)

VOCAB (REMIX) (1994, RUFFHOUSE / COLUMBIA)

FU-GEE-LA (1996, RUFFHOUSE / COLUMBIA)

READY OR NOT (1996, RUFFHOUSE / COLUMBIA)

KILLING ME SOFTLY WITH HIS SONG (1996, RUFFHOUSE / COLUMBIA)

BOOTLEG VERSIONS (1996, RUFFHOUSE / COLUMBIA)

READY OR NOT (CLARK KENT / DJANGO REMIX) / NAPPY HEADS (MAD SPIDER MIX) / DON'T CRY DRY YOUR EYES / VOCAB (SALAAM'S REMIX) / READY OR NOT (SALAAM'S READY FOR THE SHOW REMIX) / KILLING ME SOFTLY WITH HIS SONG (LIVE AT THE BRIXTON ACADEMY) / NO WOMAN, NO CRY (REMIX WITH STEVE MAR-